LIFE IN CHRIST

STUDIES IN BIBLICAL THEOLOGY

LIFE IN CHRIST

THÉO PREISS

Translated by
HAROLD KNIGHT

SCM PRESS LTD
56 BLOOMSBURY STREET
LONDON

The English version of selected chapters from

La Vie en Christ
(Delachaux et Niestlé, Neuchâtel 1952

First published 1954

Printed in Great Britain by
Robert Cunningham and Sons Ltd.
Longbank Works, Alva

CONTENTS

PUBLISHER'S NOTE

THE essays selected for this volume have been taken from *La Vie en Christ* published by Delachaux and Niestlé, of Neuchâtel and Paris, in 1952. They represent studies in the New Testament made by the late Théo Preiss, and constitute a unity in so far as the author's central interest is Christology. The author was a pastor of the French Reformed Church. Roger Mehl, Professor of Philosophy at Strasbourg University, writes of him: 'if he had lived, he would surely have given us a theology of the New Testament whose unity would have consisted in the idea of juridical mysticism, which binds together the fundamental ideas of justice, justification, witness, ambassador, pledge, seal, etc.'

I

JUSTIFICATION IN JOHANNINE THOUGHT[1]

A TRADITION going back to Clement of Alexandria emphasizes the spiritual character of the Gospel of John as the feature which distinguishes it from the three fleshly Gospels. The aged Clement was certainly accurate in his insight. But the exact sense of the word 'spiritual' should have been made clear. From Heracleon to Rudolf Steiner, gnostic commentators have seen in the spiritual Gospel the confirmation of their most audacious speculations; Neoplatonist mystics have read it in the light of the word λόγος, so iridescent, ambiguous and seductive; Fichte found in it the proof of all his idealism. Orthodox theology too has seen in the Prologue the key to the Gospel and has concentrated its essence into those wonderfully profound words: the logos became flesh. Finally, liberal criticism, using this metaphysical Gospel as a set-off to a Marcan Gospel considered as terrestrial and historical, forgetting the real meaning of the Incarnation by focussing its attention too exclusively on a metaphysical Logos radiant in glory and but thinly disguised as a historical figure, has seen in John either a speculative mind or at least a mystical soul soaring far above earthly realities. Hence there has been much talk about the Philonism of John. Today it can scarcely be said that the search for the spiritual sources of the Logos theology has been a marked success. Bousset was inclined to look in the direction of Hermetic mysticism and gnosis, Bauer and Bultmann in that of Mandean gnosis, Odeberg reads John in the light of early mystical Jewish writings, while Burney, Billerbeck, Büchsel and Schlatter—that outsider of genius—have shown in detail how thoroughly Palestinian is John in his Aramaic style and Rabbinic turns of expression. Schweitzer, who in many respects carried liberal theses to extremes, placed John even later than Ignatius and regarded him as the classic example of the Hellenization of

[1] First published in *Hommage et Reconnaissance*, a collection of studies which appeared on the occasion of the sixtieth birthday of Karl Barth, Cahiers théologiques de l'Actualité Protestante, hors-série No. 2, Neuchâtel and Paris, 1946, pp. 100-118.

Pauline mysticism into a species of mysticism of the divine.[1]

Without entering too deeply into a complicated discussion I would like to approach the Johannine problem from a standpoint which so far as I am aware has never yet been adopted. If this has not been done the reason is that the Gospel has almost universally been read in the light of the Prologue. By noting that the Prologue is only a portal, Harnack had already protested without great success against this prejudice. People talk as if the Prologue were the gold coin and the Gospel which follows simply the small change! This perspective, while not wholly false, is at least one-sided. Now the Johannine problem is not one which can be solved by considering it from one point of view only. For the thought of John has something elusive about it. In a style of grandiose monotony, it develops a few unchanging themes: Father, Son, love, life and death, light and darkness, truth and falsehood, judgment, witness. Looked at closely, its poverty is extreme, like those melodies of only three or four notes. And yet on this reduced keyboard we hear a music of infinitely varied harmonies, each note evoking so many reverberations that even the most attentive ear cannot capture them all at once. To analyse the themes in succession would be a desperate and indefinite procedure. It would be impossible to expound this thought along a straight line; that method would involve not only wearisome repetitions but the final result would be a shapeless caricature. One might as well try to adapt a helix to a straight line! All these themes are curiously interwoven with each other: none of them is capable of being analysed and explained in isolation. To say that this thought is too organic to allow of its truncation is perhaps correct but certainly inadequate. Rather, it seems to me, the difficulty of Johannine thought lies in its very simplicity. And this simplicity is not just any kind of simplicity. It arises rather from a strict convergence of all the themes towards the Person of him whose speeches, delivered in a mysterious monotone, culminate in those sovereign formulae: 'I am the light of the world . . . the resurrection, and the life. . . .' It is this convergence, this Christo-centric character, which makes this thought

[1] As regards the present state of Johannine problems, I can only refer to the fine volume, relatively complete, and very sound in judgment, of Ph.-H. Menoud, *L'Evangile de Jean d'après les recherches récentes*, Cahiers théologiques de l'Actualité Protestante, No. 3, Delachaux et Niestlé, Neuchâtel, 1943.

so resistant to any systematic analysis. With its multiple fugitive nuances, Johannine thought is as simple and elusive as the play of light and shade with which the sun's rays, shining through the trees on a hot summer's day, delight to pattern the ground.

Yet there is one aspect of Johannine thought which, while not being divorced from the whole, seems to me to afford a more coherent system of ideas. The reason for that is doubtless its less 'mystical' character. This aspect has been strangely neglected by exegetes and still more so, if that is possible, by those who have tried to give a bird's eye view of Johannine thought: I mean the juridical aspect. It is an elementary, evident fact and so simple that I feel inclined to apologize for making of it the object of a study, that juridical terms and arguments are notably frequent in the Gospels and Epistles—the Christ who is sent, witness, judge, judgment, accuse, convince, Paraclete. Even terms of a rather mystical character, like light and truth, reveal if considered from this standpoint a very marked juridical emphasis: truth is contrasted less with error than with falsehood, and less with falsehood in general than with false witness: and Jesus is the light which judges, and sheds light, as we say, in this dark and sinister world.

If this whole aspect of Johannine thought has always been overshadowed or even completely disregarded, it is because John has been made to live on a reputation which, like all reputations, is as tenacious as it is over-systematized: his reputation as a mystic. But if his message includes as well a marked juridical side, a problem arises similar to that (over which so much ink has been spilt) which concerns Pauline theology, viz., the connexion between the juridical and the mystical tendencies, some considering the former as central, others like Heitmüller, Wrede, Bousset, Schweitzer, deciding in favour of the latter. And the problem will be so much the more fascinating because John seems not to know the doctrine of justification in its Pauline form and uses a definitely original terminology. The terms 'justification' and 'justify' are absent from John and grace is found only in the Prologue (1.14, 16, 17), without direct connexion with the manner in which salvation is acquired. 'Faith' is found only once and then in the Epistle (I John 5.4). It would

be wrong to conclude from this that John is not aware of the
theme of salvation by faith: he uses the verb 'to believe' as
copiously as could be desired. But in view of these facts, it ought
no longer to be possible to make the theology of John dependent
on that of Paul, especially as the mystical terminology of John is
different from that of Paul. John does not know the formulae
'in Christ', 'the Body of Christ', the verbs in σύν, 'to die with
Christ', 'to rise again with Christ', and his terminology is too
powerfully original for us to suppose that it could have reached
him through the channel of a diffused and banal Paulinism of the
second half of the first century.

Furthermore it would be sufficient to compare the Johannine
writings with the Deutero-Pauline ones to settle the question:
the Paulinism of the Epistle to the Ephesians (if this is not by
the Apostle) is of a clearly defined type; one can discern a precise
kind of Paulinism in the Pastoral Epistles, a diffused Paulinism
in First Peter, a vulgarized and distorted Paulinism in the Epistle
of James. Above all there is one author who in time and space
and mode of thought is very near to John and yet in whose
writings one can demonstrate with real exactness to what extent
he is dependent on the Apostle Paul: even if he did not quote
him, Ignatius of Antioch would betray on each page his kinship
with Paul. His letters bristle with Pauline turns of phrase and
are fed with many of the motifs of his mysticism concerning life
in Christ. It is possible to discern with precision how Ignatius
has at one and the same time both assimilated and distorted the
thought of the apostle. He has understood and retained just so
much as it was possible for a Christian Hellenist to do: the
mysticism of the life in Christ, of the Church as the Body of
Christ. But he has detached this from the remainder and has left
aside Paul's eschatology and doctrine of justification.

By contrast with these real Paulinisms, the so-called Paulinism
of the Johannine writings has no more solidity than a ghost. In
short, it is no more than a by-product of that vast Hegelian or
Deutero-Hegelian mythology which insisted on tracing the
evolution of primitive Christianity in a unilinear way: since John
writes after Paul he must at all costs stem from him! Now the
very general arguments which it has been found possible to
adduce prove only one thing: that John writes in a situation

which is no longer that of the Pauline churches, and this result gets us nowhere, since nobody wants to gainsay that John wrote towards the end of the century. In the Epistle the problem of the law is so completely superseded that John feels obliged to remind the gnostics, with their marked indifference towards the moral life, that sin is ἀνομία[1] and at least in his formulae to adopt a certain attitude of legalistic moralism. In the Gospel Jesus often opposes the Jewish law, but the problem of the validity of the law is seen only in a Christo-centric perspective: the Pauline problem, which concerns its relevance to the *via salutis* of the Christian and the life of the Church, is at any rate left in the shade. The fact is that the problems implied in Paul's struggle against the Judaic Christians are now simply a thing of the past. And I should rather be inclined to suppose that this result was due less to a victory on the part of Paul than to a cessation of the fight through a lack of combatants. From the year 70 Judaic Christianity has its back broken. It will be able to survive only peripherally, while the churches of the Dispersion already include a large majority of Gentile Christians. The problem of the Jewish law will now be less an internal problem than a problem of apologetics as between the Church and the Synagogue. Such is the situation between the year 70 and the year 100. It is just at that time that John is writing his Gospel and Epistles. But if his thought takes shape in this post-Pauline period, it is not dependent on Paul either in its form or content.

Thus the juridical aspect of Johannine thought will not be centred on the problem of the law. Moreover it might be argued that the scope of the Pauline doctrine of justification has been narrowed down as a result of the fact that it has been interpreted almost exclusively as an answer to the question of the validity of the law. If the most recent of the champions of the mystical thesis, Albert Schweitzer, was able to consider the doctrine of justification by faith as a crater on the outskirts of the volcano of the apostles' mysticism, as a polemical theory and as somewhat *opus alienum*, the fact is that for long this doctrine had been reduced to what pietism and rationalism had made of it: viz. its subjective and individualistic aspect. Not all the personages of this drama of justification were still known: the accuser Satan

[1] I John 3.4.

had been forgotten. In particular the drama had become a non-temporal and personal interior affair, detached and isolated from the great cosmic drama of the coming of the Kingdom and its righteousness, and of the victory over Satan. Is it not significant that exegesis still fails to recognize that the parable of the Wicked Judge (Luke 18.1-8), just as much as its twin sister concerning the Pharisee and the tax-gatherer, treats of justification, but of its objective aspect, of the great clash between God and his elect on the one hand and Satan and his partisans on the other?

Schweitzer very properly realized that Pauline mysticism about dying and rising again with Christ was the normal and necessary climax to the eschatology of Paul and of Jesus himself. But this luminous insight of his was clouded by difficulties and pseudo-problems because he did not appreciate the close tie which in the whole of primitive Christianity unites eschatology and justification. Is not eschatology as a whole centred around God's judgment on the world? And will it not always include as a consequence an absolutely essential juridical aspect? And will not the central personage of this conflict between God and the prince of this world be the Judge, the Son of Man? All that Paul says about justification is but an integral part of what one might call, for want of a better term, the cosmic conflict. In this connexion I can only mention apart from Luke 18.1-8 the grandiose vision of the celestial court of justice which forms a climax to the process of justification (Rom. 8). If we wish to overcome our difficulty in appreciating the true dimensions of this doctrine we must break this age-long habit which goes back perhaps beyond the Reformation to the second century and which one-sidedly emphasizes the purely individual and subjective aspect of this important doctrine. But we are not here concerned to show how this distortion has impoverished the biblical kerygma and obscured its splendid unity. Let us simply point out that it has unduly exaggerated the difference between Paul and John. For Johannine thought puts before us precisely this cosmic and objective aspect of the great conflict.

Before sketching out in global perspective the shape of this celestial and terrestrial drama, let us summarily analyse its constituent elements. We will begin by discussing the terms 'witness' and 'to witness'. Not only are they of unusual frequency but they obviously play an essential part.

If we wish to catch their precise connotation we must not at first distinguish too sharply between their juridical and their religious uses: that would be to decide *a priori* that the religious usage is merely figurative.[1]

The only texts in which the verb 'witness' has the merely vague sense of 'solemnly declaring' are 4.44 and 13.21. Everywhere else both verb and noun connote an act that is at one and the same time religious and juridical, conceived in the framework of a contest in law.

In 8.17 allusion is made to the juridical principle of Deut. 17.6, 19.15, which requires two or three witnesses: 'Thou bearest witness of thyself; thy witness is not true. Jesus answered and said unto them, Even if I bear witness of myself, my witness is true: for I know whence I came and whither I go. Ye judge after the flesh; I judge no man. Yea, and if I judge, my judgment is true; for I am not alone, but I and the Father that sent me. Yea, and in your law it is written, that the witness of two men is true. I am he that beareth witness of myself, and the Father that sent me beareth witness of me . . .' (8.13-18). Here it might be supposed that Jesus uses the juridical categories of witness, witnessing and judgment merely to answer the accusation of false witnessing levelled by the Pharisees. But in other connexions the Johannine Christ has resort spontaneously to these themes. In the solemn monologue which crowns the interview with Nicodemus he declares that inasmuch as he is the Son of Man he is the sole eyewitness of the heavenly world (3.11-13) and explains later that he does not wish to be the judge which condemns, only the Son who saves, but that being the light he provokes judgment: those who believe come to the light which reveals that their works are good, those who do not believe evade it lest their works should be revealed.[2] A little further (3.32-33) we read that he who comes from above 'what he hath seen and heard, of that he beareth witness; and no man receiveth his witness. He that hath received his witness hath set his seal to this (another juridical

---

[1] That is done in an article, which is in other respects sound, by Strathmann in the ThWNT.

[2] ἐλεγχθῇ: juridical term like 16.8.

expression) that God is true. For whom God hath sent speaketh the words of God. . . .' The close connexion between witnessing and the One who is sent can be clearly perceived. The Son of Man is sent from above to be the ambassador as rabbinical law understands the term: the ambassador is to be identified with the one who sends him; he is the witness who, because he has seen and heard the Father, has all the authority of a plenipotentiary. After having announced the judgment and the resurrection which he will accomplish inasmuch as he is the Son of Man, Jesus declares (5.30): 'I can of myself do nothing: as I hear, I judge: and my judgment is righteous because I seek not mine own will but the will of him that hath sent me. If I bear witness of myself my witness is not true. It is another that beareth witness of me; and I know that the witness which he witnesseth of me is true. Ye have sent unto John and he hath borne witness unto the truth. But the witness which I receive is not from man. . . . But the witness which I have is greater than that of John: for the works . . . bear witness of me that the Father hath sent me. . . .' Then Jesus affirms that he is the sole witness who has seen and heard the Father, that the Scriptures bear witness of him (v. 39), that he does not receive glory from men,[1] that the Jews have not the Word and the love of God in them (vv. 38, 42), that Jesus will not accuse them before the Father: that it is Moses who will accuse them, he in whom they have set their hope (vv. 45, 46).

Thus here we have a whole series of interconnected themes: Jesus is the witness of the heavenly world; as such he is Judge of the end. But he does not intend to be the accuser of the Jews. Their *kategor*—it is well known that the Greek juridical term passed into the juridical and religious language of the Jews at the same time as its opposite συνήγορος or παράκλητος—will be Moses, he whom they believe to be their defending counsel, who will intercede at the judgment day. Jesus returns to these themes in his last words addressed to the Jews (12.35-36, 44-50): 'I judge him not. . . . For I come not to judge the world but to save the world. He that rejecteth me, and receiveth not my sayings, hath one that judgeth him: the word that I spake, the same shall

---

[1] It could be shown that glory and honour have a strong juridico-social nuance in John: prestige, authority and dignity in the eyes of men or in the sight of God.

judge[1] him in the last day. For I spake not from myself; but the Father which sent me, he hath given me a commandment what I should say. . . .'

Is it a mere coincidence that these four groups of texts or chapters 3, 5, 8, 12, gravitate around the title of Son of Man? It is consistent with classic Jewish eschatology and with that of Jesus according to the Synoptics that the Son of Man should be the central personage of the last judgment. He will be the Judge at the end. But he will also be the Paraclete before the Father, because he is the righteous One who died for the sins of the world (I John 2.1). And at this very moment witnessing to the Father he exercises judgment by his Word. Like the prow of a boat cleaving the waters to right and to left, he constrains men to declare themselves for or against him. Hence his judgment is both future and present. The process of judgment unfolds itself both on earth and in heaven: the witness who has come from heaven, to whom God himself, his works, the Scriptures, and John the Baptist, bear witness—he who will become the object of the world's attack (first concealed then open), is the One who is about to be condemned by men. But he does not cease to bear witness to the world that its works are evil (7.7); he does not need that anyone should tell him what is in man: he knows himself what is in man (2.25), because he is the Judge who is light and who sheds light (3.21). Before the court of Annas Jesus behaves as a witness (18.23) and before that of Pilate (18.37) he affirms that he has come into the world to bear witness to the truth. The truth is that the world is condemned and that he whom it is engaged in condemning is the sole righteous and true man. In the course of this gigantic juridical contest, of which the earthly career of Jesus consists, other figures emerge, notably John the Baptist, the eyewitness,[2] those who have heard him (3.28) and the crowd which bears witness to the raising of Lazarus (12.17).

---

[1] 'Judge' means here 'condemn': the word will rise as an accusing witness just as the men of Nineveh and the queen of the south will judge the present generation (Matt. 12.41-42; Luke 11.31-32).

[2] 1.32, 34; cf. 1.7, 15, 3.26. I suppose that in 1.15 he who comes after me, re-translated into Aramaic, *athe bathrai*, means 'he who followed me, my disciple'. John has avoided translating by ἀκολουθεῖν both in order to keep the paradoxical pun with 'was before me', and also not to insist on the fact exploited polemically by the Baptist's disciples that Jesus was the latter's disciple.

After the resurrection the contest goes on: in face of the hostile world, the witness *par excellence* will be the Spirit. He bears witness with the water of Baptism and the blood of the crucified; and these three are one; the Spirit is like the Son and the Father, truth itself (I John 5.6). The witnessing Spirit makes the disciples witnesses before the world (15.26-27).

And thereupon John unfolds a whole theology of the interior and exterior witness of the Spirit which can only have meaning when it is seen against the background of the quarrel between the world and believers which is developed both before the inner tribunal of the believer and the outer tribunal of the world (I John 5.4-11).

But to appreciate properly this new phase of the earthly conflict and its connexion with the conflict of Jesus, we must view the drama from the celestial and cosmic plane. The Johannine kerygma is rather reserved at this point. But what it does disclose is quite clear. At the moment when the Son of Man accepts his glorification, that is, is willing to be buried in the darkness of condemnation and death, and when the heavenly voice says in confirmation 'I have both glorified it and will glorify it again' (12.23, 28), Jesus declares: 'Now is the judgment of this world; now shall the prince of this world be cast out. And I, if I be lifted up from the earth, will draw all men unto me' (12.31, 32).

This text alone would be sufficient to explode the current prejudice which supposes that judgment for John is something purely interior and immanent and spiritual, that he has interiorized the primitive eschatology of Jesus and expects of the future only the continued presence of the Spirit. In point of fact the quarrel includes a transcendent aspect and a last judgment. But the fact is that John is very reserved about the transcendent world as about the future. He has quite simply taken very seriously the truth that only the Son of Man knows the life of the world to come and that he forbids apocalyptic speculation about this world of the beyond. Yet the few glimpses of the beyond which he permits suffice to show us that eschatology like everything else is severely concentrated on Christology. In the Son of Man, the future Judge, judgment is already mysteriously present.[1] At the very moment when the Son of Man accepts

[1] 3.14-21, 5.22-36, 9.39, 12.44.

death, there takes place in the presence of God the decisive event: Satan is cast out. He whose name means 'accuser' is banished from the divine presence.[1] That is the judgment of this world. The dominion of Satan is shattered. This text could have no better commentary than that of the apocalyptic hymn (Rev. 12.10-12): 'Now is come the salvation, and the power, and the Kingdom of our God, and the authority of his Christ: for the accuser of our brethren is cast down, which accuseth them before our God day and night. And they overcame him because of the blood of the Lamb and because of the word of their testimony. . . .' Can it be maintained that because this event is considered as past the Apocalypse has spiritualized and interiorized eschatology? The hymn goes on to warn men that the devil has descended to the earth to vex it in anger knowing that his time is short. Similarly the Gospel of John knows that Satan will continue to work on earth. There will be a tragic but provisional disjunction between the heavenly and the earthly series of events. But the quarrel which is to issue in the condemnation of Jesus is accompanied by that which ends in the condemnation of Satan the Accuser. And with his prophetic vision the Johannine Christ— and John too—sees transcendent and future events already contained in earthly and actual events. The Son of Man exalted on the Cross and at the same time paradoxically raised to the glory of the Father will take the place of the Accuser to reign as Intercessor, as Paraclete. Paraclete before God, he the Just, is the propitiation for the sins of the whole world (I John 2.1). Hence he will be able to draw all men unto him (12.32).

How will he do so? By the Spirit, until the day of his final advent for the general resurrection and the last judgment. Is it not significant that the function of the Spirit is regularly described in John more than in the rest of the New Testament in juridical terms? He is the Paraclete, he bears witness; he convicts the world of sin, of righteousness, and of judgment. He is the witness *par excellence*: he is the truth as opposed to false witness. If exegetes have not quite known what to make of the Spirit-Paraclete it is because it has not been realized that he has meaning only within the framework of the cosmic conflict. Even in

[1] The synoptics give us the very precious parallel: 'I have seen Satan fall like lightning from heaven' (Luke 10.18).

Jewish thought a precise juridical role is assigned to the Spirit. The Testament of Judah (ch. 20) is quite clear on this point: 'Know then my children that two spirits haunt man: the spirit of truth and the spirit of error. And in the midst is the understanding intelligence which inclines to whatever side it pleases. And both truth and error are written in the heart of man. And the Lord knows all things. And at no time can the works of man be hidden from him for they are written on his very bones in the Lord's eyes. And the Spirit of truth bears witness and accuses of everything, and the sinner is on fire in his heart and cannot lift his face to his judge.' Not only do we find here literally reproduced the Johannine pair, spirit of truth—spirit of error, and that in the context of judgment, but it can be clearly seen how the two sides of the trial are articulated: to the tribunal of God corresponds the tribunal in the heart of man. The Spirit is the witness of God in man. He is the accuser who reveals to him his sins. It seems paradoxical but it is quite normal when one considers it; the spirit of error, evidently the delegate and witness of Satan the heavenly accuser, does not here play the part of the adversary. For it is a question here of the sinner in an unrepentant state, when the spirit of error is seductive. Similarly in John 16.7 ff the Spirit of truth will convict the world of sin of righteousness and of judgment. It plays the part of accuser before the world so as to persuade it of the righteousness of him who has just been condemned by the world. But as soon as man has received the truth in faith, the roles are reversed: the Satanic spirit of error will seek to accuse him and to awaken in him doubt and fear, while the Spirit of truth as Paraclete will witness to him of the certainty of the love of God. In this context one can better understand the very precise sense of these passages of the Epistle. 'Hereby shall we know that we are of the truth, and shall assure our heart before him, whereinsoever our heart condemn us; because God is greater than our heart and knoweth all things. Beloved, if our heart condemn us not, we have boldness toward God; and whatsoever we ask, we receive of him (3.19-22). Herein is love made perfect with us, that we may have boldness in the day of judgment. . . . There is no fear in love; but perfect love casteth out fear, because fear hath punishment; and he that feareth is not made perfect in love (4.17-18). Hereby know we that we abide

in him, and he in us, because he hath given us of his Spirit (4.13).
And hereby we know that he abideth in us, by the Spirit which
he gave us' (3.24). Hence the faithful Christian must be sceptical
of his religious experiences, must try the spirits and judge
whether they are of God, for many pseudo-prophets have gone
out into the world. Every spirit which does not confess Jesus is
the spirit of antichrist who is already in the world. 'Ye are of
God, little children, and have overcome them; because greater
is he that is in you than he that is in the world. . . . We are of God:
he that knoweth God heareth us. He who is not of God heareth
us not: by this we know the spirit of truth, and the spirit of error'
(4.1-6). The witness of the spirit in man is the witness of God
himself. 'He that believeth on the Son of God hath the witness in
him: he that believeth not, God hath made him a liar; because
he hath not believed in the witness which God hath borne
concerning his Son' (5.6-10).

Behind all these texts and in Johannine thought in general, we
see manifested the two aspects of the debate: on the one hand the
judgment before God, on the other the verdict of the inner
tribunal within man and the hostile verdict of the world, which
without having been able to convict Jesus of sin (8.46) judges on
appearances and according to the flesh and refuses to make a
righteous judgment (7.24). The world will hate the disciples,
will persecute them as it persecuted the Master (15.20), will
banish them from the synagogue and will attempt to kill them
too for the glory of God (16.1-2). But in the course of these
trials at the end of the times, the Spirit himself will come to witness to Jesus, will be literally their Paraclete before the tribunals
and will make them witnesses (15.26-27). He will convict the
tribunal of the world concerning sin, righteousness and judgment;
of sin because they have not believed on me; of righteousness
because I go to my Father and you will see me no more; of
judgment because the prince of this world hath been judged . . .
the Spirit of truth will lead you into all truth (16.8-13). This
truth has nothing of the character of gnostic revelation about it.
Its essential content, as is seen in the reply of Jesus to Pilate, is
the justification of Jesus, that he will be and is already justified
and glorified, that already he has overcome the world (16.33) and
that with and in him, his own will be and are already justified and

glorified and triumphant. And in all that, is there not an impressive affinity with the Synoptic texts where Jesus declares that, dragged before the tribunals, the disciples will hear speaking for them and in them the Spirit of the Father as a testimony to those who accuse them? And this last phrase, 'as a testimony', which is found both in the tradition of Mark and in that of the Logia (Matt. 10.18) shows indeed that these earthly judgments are decisive for the last judgment: those who will have received the disciples and their witness will have received the Son and the Father himself, those who will have rejected them will have pronounced their own condemnation. And the Son of Man will confess before the heavenly tribunal those who have confessed him before men, will deny those who have denied him. In the Synoptics, as in John, the Spirit will therefore be the Paraclete of the faithful before the tribunals of the world, the Son of Man their Paraclete at the last judgment.

But let us return to John. Thanks to the unanimous testimony which the three witnesses, the water, the blood and that witness *par excellence*, the Spirit, bear to the faith of the Christian, John can say that faith is the victory which has overcome the world (I John 5.4-8). As in John 16.33, where Bultmann, who however does not take into account these juridical elements,[1] has noted very justly that to conquer means to emerge victorious and justified from a debate, it is here a question of the justification of Christ and of believers. These are the last words bequeathed to the disciples, 'I have overcome the world.'

This vision of the great contest which I have attempted to outline could and should be made more precise at more than one point. If it constitutes the structural ensemble of Johannine thought then the Johannine problem as a whole must be reconsidered. Since I cannot undertake that task here I will confine myself to emphasizing some of the most important consequences of the essential role of the cosmic conflict.

In the first place the Spirit-Paraclete is by no means an isolated element: he is essential and integral to this eschatological strife.

---

[1] R. Bultmann, *Das Johannesevangelium*, pp. 434-435. Cf. for example Rev. 12.11 and Rom. 3.4 and 8.37. It would be very interesting to compare John with Rom. 8 where we find 'the two spirits', 'the two Paracletes', 'be persuaded', 'conquer'.

While Jesus was on the earth he was in a twofold sense the Paraclete of his own: in God's presence where already he made intercession for them,[1] and before the world where he 'kept' them.[2] Now that he is exalted to heaven, his own will be able to pray in his name and invoke his intercession with the Father.[3] In virtue of his sacrifice he the sole just man who has died for the sins of the whole world can without qualification make intercession for the world.[4] The function of the earthly Paraclete has now devolved upon the One who is sent in the second place. As the Son had borne witness, had sought to convict the world of sin (3.20), had guided his own into the truth (14.6), the Spirit will continue this work by bearing witness to him (15.26), by convicting the world of sin and by leading the disciples into all truth. Sent by the exalted and glorified Son or, at his prayer, by the Father, he will be his witness. Like the Son he will not speak of himself: he will speak only what he has heard. And since the glorified Son has as his own all that the Father possesses (16.15), and since all judgment, the power of life and death, is remitted to the Son of Man (5.21, 27), he is quite naturally also the sovereign Disposer of the Spirit.[5] Thus in every way the Spirit-Paraclete appears as closely linked to the figure and functions of the Son of Man. He is co-relative with the Son and the indispensable witness to him.[6] There is no trace of a competition between a primitive eschatology of the Son of Man as Judge, and a spiritualized eschatology of the inner presence of the Spirit. Besides, the Paraclete, continuing the prophetic function of the Son of Man, will declare things to come (16.13). If it is said that he will remain eternally with the disciples the fact is that he will give them, up to the Parousia and in the day of judgment, that boldness which allows them to lift their face to their Father.[7] Furthermore, John is conscious of living in the last hour.[8] This hour has drawn nearer than when Paul was alive: the antichrist has already come into the world (I John 4.3). If John had not himself looked

---

[1] John 17. See also Luke 22.31 and 23.34.   [2] John 6.39, 7.12, 10.28, 18.8-9.
[3] John 14.13-16, 16.23-26.   [4] I John 2.1; John 1.29, 17.19; I John 3.5.
[5] Hence the texts seem to me to incline quite clearly towards the thesis of the Western Church which confesses the procession of the Spirit *filioque*.
[6] That is why the coming of the Spirit is strictly bound up with the departure and exaltation of Jesus. Cf. John 7.39, 16.7, 20.22.
[7] I John 2.28, 3.3, 3.21, 4.17.
[8] I John 2.18.

forward to experiencing the Parousia, the rather laboured explanation of the editors on the subject of his death (John 21.22-23) would be unintelligible. But he cherishes such a serene certitude that the death and exaltation of Jesus have gained the victory and is so careful not to stray away into gnostic and apocalyptic speculations with regard to the when and how of the Parousia, that he remains extremely reserved. On this point as on others does not Johannine thought show itself to be in remarkable conformity with the most ancient and certain data of the Synoptic tradition?

Who is the central personage in this conflict? The Logos? Because it has insisted on reading the whole Gospel through the gateway of the Logos-Prologue it is quite likely that orthodox and liberal exegesis have considerably modified the true meaning of Johannine theology. In fact the title Logos only serves to translate into Greek the dignity and the function of the pre-existing Son of Man who was associated with the work of creation and the Mediator of all revelation prior to the Incarnation. The description in a way constitutes no more than a preamble. Afterwards it does not enter into the theme. The title which Jesus himself prefers and remarkably enough, as in the Synoptics, is found only on his lips—is that of Son of Man.[1] Do we not see there another proof, indirect but very substantial, of the definitely ancient character of the Johannine tradition?

Another point which we can define more exactly is the origin and meaning of Johannine mysticism. It flows like that of Paul from life in the Spirit. Now there is nothing more juridical than the figure and the functioning of this Spirit. On this point John is even more precise than Paul. And another significant fact is also usually forgotten: in John there is no trace of pneumatic phenomena: visions, ecstasies, glossolaly. On the contrary we find a sobriety which would be almost arid and abstract if we did not feel behind it the breath of a throbbing hidden life. It is now obvious that the term mystic will have to be rendered more precise, and greatly limited, if it is to be still useful to us. Without here going into a problem which is complicated and delicate we can however emphasize two facts.

In the first place the formulae suggestive of mystical immanence

[1] John 12.34 is no exception.

so typical of Johannine language are regularly intermixed with juridical formulae. As the three witnesses are one (I John 5.7) the Father and the Son are one in their witness. Jesus reveals himself to be one with the Father as a result of the strict fidelity with which he waits upon him and utters his words and performs his task as ambassador and witness. There is of course a sort of ontological unity of eternal reciprocal immanence as between the Father and the Son. But it *coincides* with the bond formed by the obedience of a witness—a bond which has the character of something severely juridical and almost military. Jesus is in the Father and the Father in him because he does the works of the Father (10.30, 37, 38). Inasmuch as he is the Son of Man sent as a witness from the height of heaven, inasmuch as he is the ambassador sealed by God (3.33, 6.27), Jesus is according to rabbinical law 'as he who sends him'. In short I see no other suitable description but that implied in the paradoxical formula: we are here faced by a sort of *juridical mysticism*. In the same way the Father and the Son are present in the witness of the second degree which is the Spirit. Through the Spirit they come and take up their abode in the hearts of believers (14, 18, 23). Through the witness of the witnessing Spirit the Father's testimony is present with his own (I John 5.10). In the love for the brethren which the Spirit inspires, God himself is present in the faithful.

Now it can be somewhat better understood that the coming of the Son to his own in his resurrection, his coming in the Spirit, and his final coming in the Parousia, are not always clearly distinguished. Through the Spirit these three events have become like the Son and the Father himself mysteriously present and contemporary with believers, at the same time as remaining truly distinct events having their place in real time.[1] In other words, time is by no means dissolved in a non-temporal mysticism which would inevitably run into docetism. Time is *conquered*, which is

---

[1] Besides we find there the cultic experience of the first Christians; in the Eucharist, for example, believers experience a cultic Parousia in which the final Parousia is foreshadowed through the Spirit who is the precursor of the Kingdom. That is very clear in John 14.23 as in Rev. 3.20 and ch. 22. The prayer *maranatha* alludes to the cultic and final advent. Similarly the Spirit in Baptism links the Christian with the crucifixion and resurrection of Jesus on the one hand and with his future glory on the other. As regards this cultic aspect I can but refer to the fine studies of O. Cullmann, *Le culte dans L'Eglise primitive*, Cah. théol. 8, Neuchâtel and Paris, 1944; *Les sacrements dans l'Evangile johannique*, Paris, 1951 E.T. *Early Christian Worship* (Studies in Biblical Theology, No. 10) 1953; *Christ and Time* (E.T.) 1951.

not by any means the same thing. Hence we get that strange interpenetration of seasons similar to what we find in the Revelation, those elusive minglings of times: 'The hour cometh and now is,' which do not at all eliminate but on the contrary underline the decisive character of these days and hours which so solemnly articulate the course of the ultimate drama. While being much more explicitly concerned with time than the Synoptics, John also brings out much more clearly the total submission of the Son to the Father: Jesus is not the disposer of these decisive hours. Whereas his more fleshly brothers can dispose of their time Jesus manifests his divinity by being like a soldier ever prepared and on the alert for the declaration of the Father's will (John 2.4, 7.7). The same will be true of the faithful: to remain in the Son is not so much an emotional intimacy but is rather in all soberness to abide in his words (15.3, 7, 10), to keep his word and his commandments, in a word, to love.

Further, this juridical mysticism seems to me to have a second source, viz. the inclusive significance of the idea of the Son of Man. From Daniel onwards this title was used to indicate a figure representing a collective entity. Pauline mysticism had sprung from the inclusive implications of the Man, of the second Adam who died and rose again to justify sinful humanity. As the grain of wheat in dying brings forth other similar grains and does not remain alone,[1] this Son of Man by his death will draw all men unto him. They will be his brothers, his God will be their God, his Father their Father (20.17). The Spirit of the Risen Lord will through the disciples assure the sinner that he is forgiven (20.22). Henceforth they are in him (I John 2.5), in the Son and in the Father, for their sins have been forgiven them because of his name (I John 2.12). If John does not employ the terms justify and justification and hardly at all the words faith and grace, he knows very well that the Father is just (17.25), that this justice like that of the Son is not a simple *justitia passiva* which condemns man but a *justitia activa* which forgives. 'If we confess our sins he is faithful and righteous to forgive us our sins, and to cleanse us from all unrighteousness' (I John 1.9). And Jesus Christ shows that he is the just man in being before God propitiation

[1] John 12.24, 32.

and Paraclete for the sinful world. Hence the faithful will do righteousness in order to be truly just as he is just, by living in love for the brethren (I John 3.7-10). In Enoch 'the just' was one of the privileged titles of the Son of Man. But John has of course like the whole of the primitive Church replaced Son of Man by Christ. In the entire Epistle and doubtless also in the Gospel, John is keenly concerned to cut the wings of a gnostic mysticism which boasts of coming from God, of having seen and known him, of being in him, and untiringly he brings it down to earth, to the incarnate Son, to the sacraments, to simple obedience to the commandments, to love for the brethren. Is this to say that John hardly took seriously the mystical terms which he uses? He means on the contrary that in the sobriety of faith and love is to be found the goal which these terms imply. But the content of these mystical formulae is strictly disciplined and their real significance is often much less mystical than appears. Thus the famous 'Have' of John can denote a possession *in spe nondum in re*, the simple blind but absolute certitude of being already heard (I John 5.15) and the mystical 'being' can denote a mode of being which is as much future as present: 'that we should be called children of God—and such we *are* . . .' 'Beloved, now are we children of God, and it is not yet made manifest what we *shall be* . . . but we *shall be* like him . . .' (I John 3.1-2).

Thus we find here as in Paul a certain mysticism implied in this eschatology and in the idea of the justification of sinners by the Man or the Son of Man. It matters little whether or not we retain the word mystic. What alone is important is to note that John confirms with remarkable precision the thought of Paul. If he is less full than Paul on the subjective aspect of justification, on the other hand he is more precise than Paul with regard to the cosmic conflict. Like his Aramaic mode of expression, his thought emerges clad in very ancient guise. At the centre of it there rises always (though John does not himself use the title) the dominating figure of the Son of Man from heaven. Already in the Synoptics we find that if the general and exoteric term was 'Kingdom of heaven' the special and esoteric term used by Jesus himself was 'Son of Man'. John reports to us a kerygma in which apocalyptic dreams are still more plainly poured away and rejected, where all is still more centred on the Son of Man. If John has stylized and polished the tradition he has done so in the sense in which Jesus did. Thus the Johannine tradition, independent of Paul as of the Synoptics, confirms the latter and is confirmed by them at all essential points.

It would however be risky to conclude from this that the Fourth Gospel has complete authenticity and integrity as a historical document. Certainly John has nothing of the speculative ethereal mystical mind about him. His Gospel and Epistle are even in many respects more fleshly than the Synoptics. But neither is he a witness in the historical sense. First and foremost he is a witness in the juridical sense. His testimony implies of course the eye-witness who has seen, heard and touched the Word of life, but in all conscientiousness he goes beyond the fidelity of a witness in court. He knows that Jesus of Nazareth, his life and his death, had no meaning for the Jews who were eyewitnesses of them and who judged according to the flesh. And the historical Jesus, divested of all dogmatic clothing, whom the moderns attempt to discover, is a pure myth springing from the *naïveté* of a century which has tried to grasp Jesus in order to make of him the king of a religion of religious personalism: it is only to be expected that the real Jesus should elude the undertaking of historical research made in this spirit of dogmatic liberalism. The flesh alone profiteth nothing; it is the Spirit which giveth life. John illuminates the facts. In themselves these facts had no coherent meaning. Even in his lifetime, the words of Jesus called for an illumination coming from the beyond. John projects on to the facts such an illumination but from a different angle. To repeat literally in the year 90 or 100, at the last hour, the words of Jesus of Nazareth would have been to be guilty of infidelity. In truth these words had meaning only as a commentary on the events of the coming of the kingdom, of the life, death, resurrection, and Parousia of the Son of Man. After the resurrection, fidelity towards Jesus consisted then in taking seriously that decisive series of events and in speaking of the past in the light of the present. When liberal critics accuse Paul and John of changing the perspective they unconsciously admit that they are seeking in the Gospel of Jesus a collection of non-temporal truths, and in Jesus another Socrates. That means failing to appreciate the dramatic and temporal character of Christian truth and making of Jesus a gnostic. We might just as well reproach Shakespeare for not having made Macbeth repeat in the second act what he said in the first. John and Paul knew, like Jesus, that the truth is nothing other than the last word in the drama of the cosmic conflict. What would have been the use of a biography? It would have redounded to the glory of Jesus himself. Now, Jesus refused to seek his own glory. He wished only to be the witness of the Father and to efface himself. In every trial one seeks to recover the facts only in order to reach the truth and to decide the litigation.

That is the object of John, the witness to the truth. And to such an extent has he made his own the testimony of Jesus that even when he speaks of himself, he speaks no longer of himself. As completely effaced and discreet as a witness should be, he nevertheless pours himself wholly into each one of his words. And a *Formgeschichte* of the Fourth Gospel would show how he has touched up his shots and mounted his film in a series of themes which are so many points of attack and concentric testimonies bearing witness that Jesus is he who gives eternal life.

The wonder of the Fourth Gospel is inexhaustible. With his utter simplicity the eagle who has written it has an enormous wing-span: his work is at once the most juridical and the most mystical that can be imagined. Clumsy, incapable of writing a paragraph in acceptable Greek, he plays on his two manuals with equal ease and mastery. He evokes the image of Jesus in the most humble and the most splendid features. The Son is only the witness who can do nothing without the Father and yet in that very fact he reveals himself to be God. This total humility is one and the same with his perfect sovereignty. One could not imagine a Christology more exalted nor more humble. This Son is brought before us, pictured as quite near and wonderfully intimate and yet he remains strangely distant. And this Gospel of love is also one of severity.

The Logos has become flesh. These few words which are uttered from heaven to earth in fact sum up the whole Johannine message if we are careful to read the latter in the light of the Gospel as a whole. But if we elaborate a doctrine of the Logos and of the Incarnation which more or less neglects the thought of justification as the early Fathers already did, then Johannine theology becomes seriously distorted. In John there is no trace of natural theology. It is precisely in order to eliminate it that—so it seems—he has extended his Christo-centric concern to the historical past and even beyond the creation. But the prologue is only the beginning of a curve which describes the drama of the great universal conflict. In forgetting this, exegesis, both ancient and modern, has opened the door to many aberrations. By means of the prologue thus isolated, stoic, neo-platonizing and mystical speculations have easily been able to gain an entry into Christian theology. At the other end the doctrine of the Spirit lost its rigour and its moderation and could only with difficulty contain the flood of mounting speculation and mysticism. The doctrine of the Trinity itself, that admirable bastion against all speculation—does it not become powerless if separated from the thought of justification and if the juridical function of the Spirit is neglected?

It is constantly maintained that if the Church of Rome can claim the backing of Peter, the Reformed Church that of Paul, the Orthodox Church can claim for itself the Johannine tradition. There is no doubt in that an element of truth. But what is certain is that John is no less than Paul, though in other terms, the witness of what is at the heart of the message of Paul as of Jesus himself: that the heavenly Judge who is to condemn us has come to die and rise again to justify his enemies and that he will return one day in glory.

Only John gives us the kerygma of Jesus and the early Church in the most restrained, naked and stylized form. Hence it is very difficult to distinguish in his Gospel between what is the witness of Jesus himself and what is the witness of John. They have become to such an extent interpenetrated and intertwined. And that was perfectly normal and legitimate since the witness of the Spirit was that of the Son and of the Father himself, and this witness of the Spirit, so far from soaring proudly to gnostic speculations beyond the incarnate terrestrial Son who was in submission to his Father, had it as his precise function to make the Son central. But if the exegete and the historian cannot detach the 'authentic' elements they can and must note that the message of the Johannine Son of Man is, in spite of all differences in style and expression, the very same as that of the Son of Man of the Synoptic Gospels.

With that same increasing concentration which caused Rembrandt in the various stages of his 'Three Crosses' to cast more and more into the background of the field of vision all secondary personages and motives, John has scorned all the luxury of picturesque colour and detail in order to concentrate his witness on one point only and to conjure up in black and white, in the thickest darkness, the features at once so radiant and so bare of him who was and remains the Light of the world.

II

LIFE IN CHRIST AND SOCIAL ETHICS IN THE EPISTLE TO PHILEMON[1]

In these few pages we do not propose to examine once more the classic aspects of the problem posed by the letter of the Apostle Paul to Philemon. Whether it was written from Ephesus, Caesarea, or from Rome matters indeed for precise biographical information about Paul and for the exact situation of the Epistle to the Colossians, but not much for the understanding of our epistle.

It is unanimously agreed today that these few lines are a little masterpiece in which Paul reveals himself unreservedly. Goguel considers that this letter is perhaps, from the point of view of style, the best of the epistles of Paul—a *chef d'œuvre* of tact and cordiality.[2]

The Tübingen school, by declaring the epistle spurious because the situation presupposed would be too romantic, has shown itself as insipidly intellectualist and dogmatic as Jerome, Chrysostom and Theodore of Mopsuesta, when they doubted its inspiration. It is true that one might well wonder why this letter could have been preserved and read in worship along with the great letters of the apostle. What was its dogmatic interest? Was it preserved only by accident, in some way tacked on to the Epistle to the Colossians, until there grew up such veneration for the apostle as demanded the careful preservation of all that came from his hand? That is possible. But it is also possible that this letter was preserved and read in the churches for a more precise reason: either because it was more or less realized that here was an incomparable model of spiritual direction, of tact and of love, or because people relished the quite new and luminous way in which Paul approaches and decides a delicate matter arising between a Christian master and slave—or perhaps for all these reasons.

Whatever be the truth of it, the presence of this letter in the

---

[1] First published in *Aux sources de la tradition chrétienne*, a symposium for M. Maurice Goguel on the occasion of his 70th birthday, Neuchâtel and Paris, 1950, pp. 171-179.
[2] *Introduction au N.T.*, t. IV, p. 423.

New Testament—a letter which is doubly personal, as regards the recipient and as regards the sender—expresses and emphasizes the fact that the authors of the New Testament did not aim at writing a Koran of impersonal doctrines and prescriptions. How often do Christians and still more those who live on the fringes of the Church require that Scripture should provide them with a code for the journey or at least a grammar for their social and political decisions? The Bible is certainly not a very manageable grammar, and it becomes sinister when it is taken as a code.

What appears at first sight as a weakness has been, and will no doubt remain in the future, its strength and greatness. No general programme, however fine and practicable, will ever realize what the Gospel proclaims: the new heavens and the new earth where righteousness will abide. *Theologia viatorum, ethica viatorum.* The Gospel penetrates systems and civilizations but is never identified with them. In particular it is more realistic than all idealisms and all so-called political realisms: for it attacks the heart of problems, the personal centre and personal relations. So long as it has not allowed itself to be contaminated by apocalyptic or evolutionary speculations the Christian hope has been characterized by the fact that the expectation of a glorious future, far from diverting the Christian from the present moment, in which he encounters his neighbour, constantly recalls him to it as to the only place where he is able to act in freedom (Matt. 25.31-46). Moreover genuinely Christian thinking does not canonize any one brand of social order in this world where all passes away. Christian aloofness from this world has made possible a more long-term and revolutionary type of action. The Christian does not cling to immediate facts but to reality.

It is precisely this very personal and concrete character which constitutes the value of the letter to Philemon. By giving less, perhaps he gives more than a treatise on social ethics. Moreover do not let us suppose that this personal letter is of a private nature. It has not been sufficiently realized (we owe the observation to Lohmeyer)[1] that this letter, while treating a very delicate question and strictly concerning only Philemon (in modern language it is a case of tact and professional secrecy *par excellence*),

---

[1] Whose commentary on Philemon is suggestive and rich: Meyer's *Kommentar*, Phil. Kol. Philemon, Göttingen, 1930, pp. 171-192.

begins and ends as an *epistle*, associating Timothy with Paul, and associating with Philemon the whole church which assembles in his house. In this we see more than epistolary formality. The profound reason for this external fact is that in the Body of Christ personal affairs are no longer private. Inversely it could be shown that it is in his most collective and impersonal pages that Paul remains highly personal: the cleavage which separates human existence into secret private life and anonymous collective life is rejected with the passing of the old aeon; the new world which is already disclosed in the Body of Christ is both personal and communal.

Hence our letter is richer in theological suggestions than is usually supposed. The commentators quite rightly note the authority, the tact, the love of Paul. They are right to see there the very heart of the apostle. But is our normal distinction between private life and theology real for Paul? His authority, his diplomatic tact, his love and even his humour all proceed from, and are governed by, one precise thought: this whole business is here seen, experienced, and decided by Paul ἐν Χριστῷ.

The formula occurs no more frequently than in the major epistles: 'in Christ' three times (vv. 8, 20, 23), twice ἐν κυρίῳ (vv. 16, 20), once εἰς Χριστόν (v. 6). But it emerges in those essential articulations (thrice in vv. 16-20) where the apostle reveals the depth of his thought. Furthermore the letter abounds in juridical and commercial formulae like 'in thy behalf', v. 13; 'that thou shouldest have him for ever', v. 15; 'put that to mine account . . . I will repay it', v. 19; 'without thy mind', v. 14; 'if then thou countest me a partner, receive him as myself', v. 17. We find there as elsewhere but in rather unexpected guise, and very confusedly, the two modes of expression of Pauline thought: the mystical and the juridical. What is the connexion between them? The classic question arises again: which of the two expresses the heart of his thought?

It is not a question of justification here. The juridical formulae express rather a certain situation existing between Paul, Onesimus and Philemon, a whole circuit of relations which seem to be both juridical and mystical. Let us try to unravel this network. It will be clearer if we first sketch out the juridical situation according to human law.

The slave Onesimus has fled from his master. It may be that the rascal has been stealing; in any event he owes his master at the present moment all the work not performed, or, if he worked elsewhere, the share of his wages due to the master. How has he got into touch with Paul? If he had been caught in a raid by one of those terrible commando assaults on slaves and had by chance met Paul in prison, it would not be at all clear why Paul could assume the right to deal with him as freely as he does. A slave who was caught was punished severely and sent back to his master. If he had taken refuge in an official asylum according to law or custom and refused to return to his master he was sold again to another.[1] This second hypothesis is also excluded.

The most plausible supposition is that Onesimus, having heard of Paul in his master's house, joined him after his flight without having been arrested. Life was terrible to slaves in flight. If there is no longer slave or master, the sponsor of Philemon can only plead. . . .

Lohmeyer suggests furthermore that Onesimus acted according to the custom, widespread in Asia Minor particularly, of the right of asylum. A worn-out slave could take refuge in certain sanctuaries like the Theseion of Athens and the temple of Artemis at Ephesus. According to right and custom the slave is protected by the god. In return he dedicates himself as slave of the god for a varying period. Onesimus may have had the idea of placing himself with Paul under the protection of the god which binds Philemon too.

The suggestion is attractive and fairly plausible. But it is only a hypothesis. It would permit us to envisage more clearly that juridical-religious background which is there in any case. What is more certain and more important is that in returning Onesimus with this letter Paul is acting in accordance with the law of the period. Whoever keeps with him a runaway slave makes himself an accomplice of a serious infringement of private law. He owes the owner the value of each day's work lost. This is what Paul solemnly undertakes to make good: 'Charge it to my account . . . I will pay.' So far the attitude of Paul is perfectly normal.

But that someone should presume to interfere with a master's

[1] Pauly-Wissowa, *Realenzyklopedie der klass. Altertumswissenschaft.*, art. 'Sklaven.'

right of ownership over his slave is strictly inconceivable. Now, this is just what Paul does—with a calm smiling authority, but with a firm commanding accent. The question whether Paul demands the official and regular release of Onesimus is debatable. Lohmeyer, contrary to the majority of authors, thinks that he does. I am not so sure. But what is difficult to dispute is that Paul gives it to be understood with all necessary clarity that he expects Onesimus to be sent home for the service of the Gospel. After all, the question of the freeing of this slave is of less concern to Paul here than in his exhortations to slaves in I Cor. 7. Paul does not seriously expect Philemon to reinstate Onesimus in his work as a domestic or field slave. It is not here a question of urging slaves to remain in their station as it is in I Cor. 7. Of course Paul writes: 'whom I have sent back to thee in his own person, that is, my very heart', but he does not say: 'receive him again'. All the phrases used affirm with the clarity desirable that Philemon should receive not the old good-for-nothing Onesimus but 'my child, whom I have begotten in my bonds'. Finally Paul states quite clearly 'receive him as myself'. The idea of returning is reduced to its spatial connotation and is overshadowed by that of Onesimus as the messenger of Paul to Philemon, a messenger in whom he intends to be really present.

We are here faced by the Jewish and Christian category of the ambassador. In the Talmud we read a dozen times the principle of law: 'the messenger (*shaliakh*) is as the one who sends him.' The mandatory, the plenipotentiary is really clad in the authority of his master. Paul sent Onesimus with Tychicus to the Church of the Colossians, 'the faithful and beloved brother, who is one of you' (Col. 4.9). Onesimus is thus already in some sort, although in the capacity of associate of Tychicus no doubt, the *apostolos* of Paul to the Church. Is he not about to become so even more specially with Philemon?

We cannot appropriately study here in detail the Jewish notion of the *shaliakh* and its role in the formation of the Christian idea of the apostle.[1] Let it suffice to emphasize the note of juridical mysticism which the idea of the emissary takes on in the thought of Jesus.[2] Emissary and substitution seem to have been for Jesus

---

[1] See Rengstorf art. Ἀπόστολος in ThWNT.
[2] Cf. the following essay of the present volume.

fundamental categories. On this point his thought is perhaps in a sense the powerful and wonderfully simple concentration of certain classical elements in Jewish thought. Here too, no doubt —in the idea of the Son of Man or true Adam mysteriously present in his emissaries—we should seek the origin and essence of the Pauline doctrine, so rich and sonorous, of life in Christ and of the Body of Christ. It would be very strange if in writing these words Paul had in mind merely the principle of Jewish law. The formula has certainly a much greater depth. The one who wrote II Cor. 5.16-20 could not have put into them less than his certainty that just as Christ identified himself with the sons of Adam by a mysterious exchange of their sin with his righteousness, each of the members of his Body gives himself to, and identifies himself with, the others.

If this is recognized then the question of knowing whether Onesimus is or is not truly the *shaliakh* of Paul becomes very secondary. For the mystical presence of Christ in his own simply overflows the category of the emissary. A word of Jesus is here decisive: 'Whosoever shall receive one of such little children in my name, receiveth me: and whosoever receiveth me, receiveth not me, but him that sent me' (Mark 9.37; cf. Matt. 10.40). To clothe a wretch is to clothe the Son of Man in one of the little ones who are his brethren (Matt. 25.40). It remains however that the Christ is specially present in his emissaries and apostles and even in the occasional 'apostles of the churches' of II Cor. 8.23. These delegates of the churches whose duty it is to take the collection to Jerusalem are called apostles (*Shelikhin*) after Jewish custom. But Paul specifies by the words 'glory of Christ' that the emissary of a church is not only a mandatory in the juridical and secular sense; for those who receive him, the head of the body is present in him with all his glory, his divine *shekinah*. The Didache also commands (4.1) that we should honour 'as the Lord him who announces the word. For where Lordship is proclaimed there the Lord is.'

In order to justify the liberty he takes, the apostle here makes use of the authority of Christ himself. He is his ambassador, his πρεσβευτής. It is of course πρεσβύτης, old man, that we find in v. 9. Bentley and others have conjectured that we should read 'ambassador' and add the epsilon. This conjecture is unnecessary. Lightfoot and Lohmeyer have established that a good number of texts, from the LXX to Eusebius, use the two words interchangeably. Theophilactus understands the word 'old man' in the two senses. All in all, Eph. 6.20 explains our text very well: 'for which I am an ambassador in chains' (cf. also II Cor. 5.20). The context and these parallels show sufficiently that Paul invokes here his authority as an ambassador. Besides, his sufferings for his master attest the authenticity of his communion with him and of his authority. In short, Paul wants to put the greatest weight into the formulae in which he identifies himself with Onesimus.

But must these formulae be understood in the strongest sense? Did Paul identify himself to this extent with Onesimus? Have we not here a rhetorical hyperbole? Let us note that inversely Paul considers it quite natural that Onesimus returning to him should serve him in place of his master (v. 13). Paul follows always the same principle: the emissary is in reality as the one who sends him. Onesimus when with Paul is the representative of Philemon and when with Philemon the representative of Paul. Especially has Paul so identified himself with his 'child' that he takes over his debts. In Roman and Greek law the father is the financial guarantor and pays the debts of the child. With a pleasant smile Paul traces with his hand the usual commercial *intercessio*: 'put that to mine account . . . I will repay.' And with a touch of gentle irony he adds in passing 'that I say not unto thee how that thou owest to me even thine own self besides'. What is the debt of Onesimus in comparison with this eternal debt?

It is clear that this curious theological accountability stems directly from that remission of all their sins which is the source of life to the members of the Church. It has been possible to suppose that in the background of our letter is implied the parable of the pitiless debtor.[1] Between the members of the Church there takes place an exchange of spiritual and material goods (Rom. 15.27; I Cor. 9.11) in which one gives oneself to the Lord and to the brethren. This *koinonia*, or communion, or participation, is both very practical and mystical.[2] Above all, this concrete life

[1] Thornton, *The Common Life in the Body of Christ*, p. 43.
[2] Cf. Barnabas 19.8: 'You will have everything in common with your neighbour

in Christ is only a consequence of the remission of sins and of justification. Without shame Paul sums up in commercial formulae: 'If then thou countest me a partner, receive him as myself' (v. 17).

How do the situation in civil law and this new situation of the life in Christ react upon each other?

In principle Paul has the right to claim the boundless services of Philemon. By Jewish custom itself the disciple owed to his master the services of a slave. *A fortiori* Philemon, the convert and initiate of Paul, will owe to him the fact that he is now a freed man of the Lord. But then, why does Paul with a subtle smile and yet the greatest seriousness comply with the legal requirement of that 'private guarantee'? Here is a type of humour which is primarily a delicate expression of tact and love and which at the same time will gently win consent and dissolve the impulse to resentment in the master, and here too we find a masterly pride in which is affirmed all the Christian liberty of the apostle. This attitude strikingly recalls that of Jesus (authentic or not) in the incident of the coin (Matt. 17.24-27). Paul submits himself to human law from love, in the measure in which he can express his Christian love and liberty. He signs his pledge. He demands nothing. Is not the apostle like his master the slave of all (I Cor. 9.19-23; II Cor. 4.5)? In the Body of Christ each serves the other (Gal. 5.13). Onesimus will serve the Lord by helping the apostle. At the same time, sent back by his master to Paul, he will permit Philemon to serve more effectively. Philemon can see in that only a magnificent opportunity of overcoming space to be with the apostle and of serving the Gospel more directly. Thus inversely Onesimus will be the emissary of Philemon. What is more, by giving him freely to the service of the Lord Philemon will possess him for ever. The formula 'that thou shouldest have him for ever' (v. 15)[1] has, as in Phil. 4.18, the commercial sense of acknowledging a receipt, a 'duly receiving'. In the new order in Christ one possesses only what one has given. Nothing gives us reason to suppose that Paul visualizes that Onesimus will remain with Philemon and resume his old tasks. He clearly

and will call nothing your own. For if you are communal in what is incorruptible how much more in corruptible things.'

[1] Deissmann, *Licht vom Osten*, 4th ed., p. 88.

expects to see him back again soon as a collaborator. The formulae which he uses are so much the more significant: 'no longer as a servant, but more than a servant, a brother beloved, specially to me, but how much rather to thee, both in the flesh and in the Lord' (v. 16). This last point, '. . . both in the flesh and in the Lord', is especially significant. Lietzmann translates, with reference to Rom. 8.11: 'both as man and Christian.' This makes impossible the dualistic social ethics which only too often are felt to be implied by the exhortations of the epistles. If Paul had wished to reinstate Onesimus in a social order which must not be changed, if he had juxtaposed life in Christ to an order of creation, and love to civil justice, he would have written something like, 'my dear Philemon, in the Lord, you are brothers, and one; in the life of the world you remain each in his place socially.' Above all Paul would have respected the master's right of ownership over his slave. In actual fact Paul does no such thing: fraternity, unity in Christ, seizes upon the relation of slave and master, shatters it and fulfils it upon quite another plane. Onesimus will be considered not merely as an equal, another member of the Church, he will be a member of Philemon's family, a full brother. Thus there remains no margin of paternalism, what we have is a total fraternity.[1]

In vain do we seek in the New Testament for a condemnation of slavery in principle. To indulge gratuitously in such declarations would have been absurd, '. . . to abolish slavery it would have been necessary to overthrow all institutions, destroy the city.'[2]

Meantime Paul says not a word about the emancipation of Onesimus. Is it because the problem is, as in I Cor. 7, relativized to the point of becoming indifferent? Or is it that Paul only wishes to leave it to Philemon to think and act spontaneously in a way that will most gladden the heart of Paul the Christian? While inclining to this last hypothesis I think it necessary to leave the matter undecided.

In any case our letter shows that the well-known exhortations

[1] As a facile apologetic thinks it right to emphasize the cruelty of the ancient world there is reason to recall statements like that of Pliny who insists that one sees in the slave not a tool but a brother who serves. It goes without saying that this formula, fine as it is, must be carefully distinguished from Pauline thought.

[2] G. Glotz, *Le travail dans la Grèce ancienne*, Paris, Alcan, 1920, p. 264.

of I. Cor. 7 and elsewhere are far from giving us the whole thought and practice of the apostle. Here we see life in Christ pierce more clearly and deeply than elsewhere a problem of social ethics. The fact that this particular case cannot be extended and generalized does not authorize us to see in it an exceptional depth of penetration. The very positive and concrete richness and fulness of Paul's social ethics are in large measure concealed by the necessity in which he found himself to suppress abuses and to be somewhat negative. Thus the passages relative to slaves in primitive Christian literature nearly all suffer from being partial and one-sided. It was constantly necessary to react against the most vulgar confusions between Christian liberty and a lazy anarchism. In 112 or 117 Ignatius writes to Polycarp (4.3), 'Let them address themselves to their service with still more zeal, for the glory of God, so as to obtain from him true liberty. Let them not be too impatient to be freed at the expense of the community: that would be to show themselves slaves of their own desires.' That proves that, in certain cases at least, the churches ransomed slave-members at the common expense. Abuses can be easily imagined, candidates for baptism streaming in. . . . To take these necessarily somewhat one-sided exhortations as a general rule and the pass-key to social morality would be a grave mistake. The New Testament is not revolutionary in the modern sense; but still less is it conservative: every social order is in fact superseded and passes away with the structure of this world. On the other hand these few lines of Paul to Philemon disclose clearly the network of new situations and the circuit of new relations which constitute the life in Christ, the life of the Church. Pauline ethics proceed not from law, nor from principles, but from this circulation of love of the new world which has invaded the old. But this circulation has nothing vague or sentimental about it: life in Christ does not mean a 'sphere of vitalism' (Deissmann), a diffuse mysticism. On the one hand this mystical life flows directly from the remission of sins, from justification of which after all it is only another expression. On the other hand, it culminates in 'a technique of Christian co-operation' (Thornton, p. 39) which is very precise and does not fear to use the most common and secular business terms. If this ethic can bring off this strange *tour de force* of being at one and the same time so juridical, so mystical and so concrete, that is because with a fine severity it is so deeply Christo-centric. It seeks only to express in daily life the unheard-of fact that in Jesus Christ all are one: in him there is no more slave nor free (Gal. 3.28). Yet this unity is reflected not in uniformity, but in a constant tactfulness towards and respect of one's neighbour. With what carefulness Paul respects the liberty of Philemon!

The same tact, authority and respect for the liberty of others could be found in many passages of the Epistles but more especially in II Cor. 8-9, where Paul approaches the delicate question of the collection. There again his guiding thought is fellowship with him who to enrich us became poor. Even in the base questions of ownership and money and at the very heart of the reign of Mammon the apostle raises the ensign of the victory of the 'new Man'.

III

THE MYSTERY OF THE SON OF MAN[1]

WE have heard much since the brilliant thesis of Wrede[2] about that Messianic secret which like an Ariadne thread runs through the labyrinthine passages of St. Mark's Gospel. Without wishing to minimize the importance of this motive, it may be pointed out that all the windings of the river of the synoptic tradition, not only Mark but also the *Logia*[3] and the special material of Matthew and Luke, recognize more or less explicitly but sufficiently clearly another secret which has all the appearance of being central in another manner.

When Jesus speaks to the crowd, he normally uses the general term kingdom of God: but with the disciples in intimate converse, at least from the decisive turning point of Peter's confession at Caesarea Philippi, his words are concentrated on the figure and destiny of the Son of Man. It would seem then that Jesus gave an exoteric teaching to the crowd and an esoteric initiation to those nearest him. It is moreover very probable that Jesus spoke of this secret with diminishing reserve in proportion as the storm grew that was to burst on him at Jerusalem.

Whatever be the truth in detail, in Mark's Gospel the theme of the Messianic secret shows very well the reality of these two concentric circles of teaching and what distinguishes them. But it expresses only the negative side of the attitude of Jesus: his absolute refusal to be proclaimed Messiah. What then is the positive element, the deep reason for this reserve?

It is his doctrine of the Son of Man. This heavenly Man of the Apocalypses, who will come at the last day to judge men with a sceptre of iron, must first of all live the wretched destiny of the Servant of Isaiah 53. Rejected by his own, he will suffer and die

---

[1] First published in the Review *Dieu Vivant* 8, 1947, pp. 17-36. The present text is a chapter taken from a work in preparation on *Le Fils de l'Homme*, a work in which I try to show that New Testament Christology and in particular the theme of the Church as the Body of Christ is already implied in the thought of Jesus. I hope I may be forgiven for the more obscure passages. The state of my health does not allow me to revise this text for separate publication.

[2] W. Wrede, *Das Messiasgeheimnis*, Göttingen, 1901.

[3] The collection of sayings of Jesus used by Matthew and Luke.

for them. There lies the mystery of the kingdom of God. And
yet he will be King. But King of the world to come.

This identity between the Son of Man as Judge, and the King
of the world to come, emerges with striking clearness in the
grandiose pattern of the Last Judgment (Matt. 25.31-46):

> But when the Son of Man shall come in his glory
>   And the angels with him,
> Then shall he sit on the throne of his glory:
>   And before him shall be gathered all the nations:
>   And he shall separate them one from another,
>   As the shepherd separateth the sheep from the goats:
>   And he shall set the sheep on his right hand, but
>   the goats, on his left.

Then shall the King say unto them on his right hand:

> Come, ye blessed of my Father,
> Inherit the kingdom prepared for you from the
>   foundation of the world.
> I was an hungred   and ye gave me meat:
> I was thirsty   and ye gave me drink:
> I was a stranger   and ye took me in:
> I was naked   and ye clothed me:
> I was sick   and ye visited me:
> I was in prison   and ye came unto me.

Then shall the righteous answer him, saying:

Lord,
> When saw we thee an hungred, and fed thee?
>   or athirst, and gave thee drink?
> And when saw we thee a stranger, and took thee in?
>   or naked, and clothed thee?
> And when saw we thee sick, or in prison, and came unto
>   thee?

And the King shall answer and say unto them:

Verily I say unto you, Inasmuch as ye ministered unto one of
these my brethren, ye ministered unto me.

Then shall he also unto them on the left hand:

> Depart from me, ye cursed, into the eternal fire which is
> prepared for the devil and his angels:
> for I was an hungred   and ye gave me no meat:
> I was thirsty   and ye gave me no drink:
> I was a stranger   and ye took me not in:
>   naked   and ye clothed me not:
>   sick, and in prison   and ye visited me not.

Then shall they also answer, saying:

> Lord, when saw we thee an hungred
>   or athirst,
>   or a stranger,
>   or naked,
>   or sick,
>   or in prison,
> and did not minister unto thee?

Then shall he answer them, saying:

> Verily I say unto you,
> Inasmuch as ye did it not unto one of these least ye did
>   it not unto me.
> And these shall go away into eternal punishment:
> But the righteous into eternal life.[1]

[1] This translation calls for a few words of explanation:

(a) Such an arrangement is essential in order to bring out the logical and poetic structure of this text. This structure has in its very simplicity a unique grandeur. It is possible that oral tradition or Matthew himself has shortened the dialogue with the condemned; but we cannot exclude the possibility that Jesus himself accelerated the rhythm of the final scene. In any case this acceleration lends to the scene with the condemned something breathless and distressing, which forms a powerful contrast with the slow-moving serenity of the dialogue with the elect.

(b) I have translated literally 'I was a stranger and ye took me in'. The verb συνάγειν expresses a precious shade of thought; it means more than receive or take in; it means at least: you have incorporated, integrated, united me with your community. In Aramaic the verb must have been *kanash* which has given *kenishtha* (Hebrew *keneseth*), the word which means synagogue and which according to K. L. Schmidt and others was used by Jesus to denote the community of the final aeon, the Church. Thus one wonders whether this verb which logically can only have a plural object does not betray in this text the inclusive and collective sense of the term Son of Man. In that case we should have to see in the terms themselves an allusion to the Church-body of the Son of Man.

(c) I have taken the liberty of translating the Greek phrase 'Inasmuch as ye did

This text does not seem to have been exploited in all its richness by modern Protestant exegetes. The exegesis of Catholic authors, like Mersch[1] for example, has better appreciated its mystical depth and views it rightly as one of the sources of the idea of the Body of Christ. Schweitzer[2] too, has grasped its importance but no more than Mersch has he appreciated the element of juridical substitution in it.

In addition the very place of the passage has caused it to be the subject of misunderstanding. Because Matthew has placed it with a fine sense of fitness right at the end of the teaching of Jesus, on the eve of the passion, at the end of the series of eschatological parables, the bad habit has been formed of speaking of the parable of the last judgment. In fact the only parabolic element is the image of the shepherd, of the sheep and the goats, v. 33, which is only an illustration given in passing and is also a fairly clear allusion to Ezek. 34. All the rest is direct language and its intention is to give an evocation, a vision of the last judgment. In consequence nothing justifies us in not taking literally the words which the Son of Man is about to pronounce from the throne of his glory.

It is important also to note how far the formal structure of the vision is simple, close-knit, and, as a result of the powerful and almost mathematical symmetry between the elect and the damned, singularly easy to grasp. And it is just as difficult to distort as it is easy to grasp it. To realize this it suffices to try it with children. Doubtless this pericope does not fall into any of the Jewish or Christian literary genres which the *Formgeschichte* method tries to disentangle: parable, allegory, paradigm, apophthegm, *nouvelle*, legend; rather it could be classified, from the point of view of form, with apocalyptic visions which have not usually a simple

it unto one of these my brethren, even these least . . .' by 'as ye *served* one of . . . these least', for the following reason: in Aramaic, Jesus could only have used the verb *abad*, which means both 'do' and 'serve'. The text shows that the essential meaning is 'serve'. The Greek verb for 'do' would require an object: the phrase 'inasmuch as ye did to one . . .' is not absolutely impossible in Greek, but not very satisfying, and it is our translations which intercalate 'it'. Now if the true sense was 'serve' any mention of the object of the action is excluded. Our hypothesis is confirmed by the fact that in their reply the condemned suddenly use the verb serve (διακονεῖν), which of course breaks the symmetry, otherwise so strict in the Greek text, but did not break it in the Aramaic original. I confess I do not see why *abad* could have been translated first by 'do', then by 'serve'.

[1] Mersch, *Le Corps mystique du Christ*, I, pp. 60-61.
[2] Schweitzer, *Die Mystik des Apostels Paulus*.

and definite structure. Nevertheless its own structure is strikingly solid, and in consequence looks as if it has been through several decades of oral tradition undistorted. The Aramaisms which we have noted can only reassure us on this point. Lastly, this eschatological vision differs from the Jewish or Christian genre of apocalyptic vision by a sobriety of feature and colour,[1] a reserve, a bareness which can come from hardly any other source but that of Jesus himself. Moreover, if one reads the Gospels by contrast with Jewish apocalypses, have not the evocations of Jesus with regard to the world to come a reserve and sobriety which is piercing?

These remarks on the form of this text lead us to emphasize a first fact relative to its content: from the moment when the Son of Man coming in his glory has sat on the throne of his glory he is no longer called Son of Man but βασιλεύς, King (vv. 34 and 40). Why this change of title in the course of the narrative? If it was due to oral or written tradition we should have, rather, according to the current tendency of tradition, the normal title of *Christos*. Thus this change does not reflect the dogmatic tendency of the Church. Besides it would be very difficult to attribute the change to conscious distortion or accident. Is it not in strict accord with the demands of the story? It is logical and necessary that from the precise moment when he is seated on the throne, and then only, the Son of Man should be called King. The title King can and must therefore, from the moment of the Parousia, succeed the title of Son of Man.

Now since it is highly likely that we are here faced by the words of Jesus himself we have thus perhaps the key to the disturbing question of the sense in which Jesus might have understood the Jewish title of Messiah-King: Jesus will be the King, inasmuch as he is Son of Man, when he returns in glory, but not before. While on earth Jesus refuses the title, at least in the politico-religious sense in which the Jews understand it. But he accepts it and even claims it for the world to come. This we think is the best explanation of the reply of Jesus before the Sanhedrin (Mark 14.62), 'I am, and ye shall see the Son of Man sitting at

[1] It is amusing to note in passing that so perspicacious a critic as C. H. Dodd (*The Parables of the Kingdom*, p. 85) can see in this text a short apocalypse in which the traditional scene of the last judgment is 'depicted in vivid colours . . .'. Where are these vivid colours? Not in the text. But its evocative pregnancy causes the reader to see the scene in vivid colours.

the right hand of power, and coming with the clouds of heaven.' Because he is the *Messias designatus*, and only *designatus*, Jesus can and must both claim and refuse the title. The reply to Pilate of John 19.36: 'My kingdom is not of this world,' has moreover the same sense: my kingdom comes in a different way from the kingdoms of this world, it comes from above not from below. This is saying in a different way that the Son of Man comes with the clouds of heaven.

And have we not there quite simply the logical origin and also the justification, given by Jesus himself, of the use in the primitive Church of the title *Kurios*? It is certain, in spite of the efforts of Bousset to assign to the cult of the Lord a Hellenistic origin, that at a very early date the primitive Church of Palestine invoked its master, raised to the right hand of God, under the Aramaean title of *Maran*, 'our Lord'. The Aramaean liturgical formula *Maranatha*, 'Lord come', is in itself an irrefutable proof. In the most ancient Christian document that we have, I Thess. 5.2, Paul alludes to the parable of Jesus (Matt. 24.43-44, Luke 12.39-40): 'For yourselves know perfectly that the day of the Lord so cometh as a thief in the night.' The phrase 'the days of the Son of Man' is translated by Paul therefore as 'the day of the Lord'. The expression 'Day of the Lord', classic in the prophets, has probably contributed to this translation. But in the thought of Paul in general, *Kurios* now denotes the dignity of the Son of Man exalted to the right hand of God (cf. Phil. 2.11).

Perhaps it will be objected that our text attributes to Jesus the royalty and lordship of God only after his Parousia as Son of Man, while the primitive Church called Jesus Christ and Lord from the moment of his resurrection. We should see there less a difficulty than a confirmation of what we have just suggested. In fact this objection can only confirm that our text is ancient, anterior to the Christology of the primitive Church, hence authentic. Besides, it only emphasizes a general fact which concerns the eschatological hope as a whole. While the Jews, John the Baptist and the disciples—and perhaps indeed Jesus himself for a time and to an extent which it would be difficult to determine—were expecting to see the events and the gifts proper to the end accomplished within a measurable period of time and without intervals of waiting (cf. Acts 1.6), the primitive Church saw itself constrained by its Lord to tear in two the traditional eschatology: on the one hand stands what has already been realized by the life, death and resurrection of Jesus, and on the other, what will only come through the Parousia. Without here going into the complex of problems set by this sudden change of perspective—and experienced by exegetes of today—we will simply note that the primitive Church did not too happily accept the idea of this bisection. Certainly one can feel many hesitations: sometimes salvation is thought to have been already attained, sometimes merely hoped for: now eternal life is present, now it is future. Through all the New Testament writings there runs the thread of a dialectic springing from the dual and paradoxical nature of this intermediate and parenthetic time when the Church is conscious of living between the old world, defeated and yet still terribly aggressive, and the world to come which has already dawned in the resurrection of Jesus and yet is still obscure and hidden from the eyes of men. The Church was able to sustain this tension and prevent a complete rupture in its eschatology only through the concept, and above all the reality, of the Holy Spirit given as a foretaste, first fruits, and pledge of the world of the resurrection still to come. In certain respects Jesus is already, by his resurrection and exaltation to the right hand of God, the King and Lord of the world. The resurrection of Jesus is the objective anticipation, the spearhead, the victorious vanguard of the general resurrection, hence of the Parousia. One can and must henceforth call Jesus King and Lord. The possible Messianic misunderstanding had now only a retrospective interest; the risk of seeing in Jesus a political Messiah was no more. Condemned to death, conquered by the authorities of Israel and Rome, he was justified by the resurrection and exalted to the right hand of God. Thus he is indeed the Messiah, the *Christos*. He is much more than the terrestrial Messiah expected by the Jews. Already he secretly reigns over all the powers which, whether they know it or not, are subject to him even in this aeon. If on the one hand salvation as a whole is still future, on the other everything is already accomplished. The apostle Paul has concentrated this dialectic of future and past in the lapidary and paradoxical formula: 'We have been saved by hope' (Rom. 8.24).

D

What the primitive Church did for the title of Messiah and the function of the Lord, it was perfectly logical that it should also do for other attributes of the Son of Man. Just as the resurrection and exaltation of Jesus—the first Christians distinguished the two events less rigorously than we have been accustomed to do since the Book of Acts[1]—were considered as an anticipation of the Parousia, other eschatological functions of the Son of Man could and even should be equally antedated. Thus already we see the Son of Man intercede at the right hand of God, as witness and Paraclete for his earthly witness Stephen, condemned by the Jews.[2] That is also why Luke or the tradition which he reproduces was able to modify the reply of Jesus to the high priest (Mark 14.62) as: '. . . from henceforth shall the Son of Man be seated at the right hand of the power of God.'[3] It was so much the easier for the first Christians to foreshadow in the resurrection-ascension the Parousia functions of the heavenly Son of Man as the latter title had not been for Jesus, like that of Messiah, the object of hesitations and difficulties. Our text alone would prove that Jesus did not consider that he should only become Son of Man at the Parousia, since the title Son of Man must be replaced by that of King as soon as its bearer is seated on the throne. Jesus does not speak only of the Son of Man as future, more than once he speaks of him as present. There is certainly a mystery about the Son of Man. But this mystery is something in the present and only its full disclosure is future. Finally, in the Jewish hope there is in this respect a difference between the title of Messiah and that of Son of Man which cannot be neglected: while because of his earthly origin the Messiah seems only to have a sort of future eternity, the Son of Man, according to the book of Enoch and 4 Esdras, is a celestial being existing prior to the creation, but kept secretly before the Lord and manifested only at the time of his advent. As this figure always implies pre-existence, we are quite justified in postulating until the contrary is proved that the same thing applies in the thought of Jesus. Jesus does not here (Matt. 25.31) speak formally of an eternal

---

[1] That is the true element in the thesis of Bertram, who maintains that originally the Church professed the ascension of the Lord from the Cross. G. Bertram, *Die Himmelfahrt Jesu vom Kreuz aus und der Glaube an seine Auferstehung*, Festgabe für Ad. Deissmann, 1927.
[2] Acts 7.56.   [3] Luke 22.69.

pre-existence but he affirms that until his final glorious manifesta-
tion the Son of Man knows a mode of existence and of presence
of a very special, secret and mysterious kind.

He will have been mysteriously present in the wretched, in his
brethren who are hungry, naked, sick, and in prison. At the time
of his Parousia the transcendent Judge, the Son of Man of
Daniel and Enoch, will reveal to all the nations, gathered together
and massed on his right hand and his left, a mystery of cosmic
proportions. This Judge whom they will think they are seeing
for the first time will be found to be one whom they have been
meeting during the whole course of their earthly lives. And they
will only come to understand this mystery when it is too late,
when already they have been judged and classified as belonging to
the right or the left. Both the elect and the damned will ask in the
greatest surprise, 'But when saw we thee hungry . . .?' and the
Judge-King will reply to the elect, 'Each time you served the least
of these my brethren, you served me.'

The history of the exegesis of this text[1] seems to show that
commentators have been somewhat hypnotized by the rather
secondary question of discovering who are the wretches and who
are the just. Luther (sermon of 1537 and *Kirchenpostille*), anxious
to set aside any synergistic explanation, sees Christians in both
groups. Calvin, who realized the link with Ezra 34.21, thinks
that the Lord is here dividing his Church: it is not a question of
pagans, but of the church which will embrace all nations. He
points out, moreover, with his usual exegetic acumen, that if the
just are recompensed it is by grace: elect and blessed of the
Father, they receive as their inheritance the Kingdom prepared
for them from the foundations of the world. Vilmar, like Luther
and Calvin, sees in the least of the brethren of Jesus the apostles
and the successors of the apostles. At first sight it seems that
this is only a variant of Mark 9.41 and of Matt. 10.40-42, where
Jesus declares that he who receives one of his emissaries receives
the Lord himself. If Matt. 25 said no more than this we should
have here only a strict application of the principle of rabbinic
law, 'the emissary is as he who sends him'. It is certain that

---

[1] W. Brandt, *Die geringsten Brüder. Aus dem Gespräche der Kirche mit Matt. 25.31-46*,
in *Jahrbuch der Theol. Schule Bethel*, Bielefeld, 1937, pp. 1-28. Brandt hardly realized
that the essential point in the text was the mystery of the Son of Man.

Jesus has often applied this principle to his emissaries and apostles, and that if we take him literally he sketched out a sort of juridical mysticism whereby the sender is present in his emissaries. But there is something more here. First, nothing suggests that the wretches were only apostles or disciples in the broad sense. Above all we know from Mark 9.37 that Jesus extended this mysticism to include children: 'Whosoever shall' receive one of such little children in my name, receiveth me: and whosoever receiveth me, receiveth not me but him that sent me (cf. also Matt. 18.5). How could children be emissaries, apostles of Jesus and of God? We have in Mark 9.37 and Matt. 18.5, as well as in Matt. 25, a vast and profound juridical mysticism, which far transcends the limits of the rabbinical principle; the Son of Man has made himself one with all those who objectively need help, whatever be their subjective dispositions. It is not said that these hungry ones, strangers, prisoners, were Christians. The Son of Man sees in any wretch his brother; and the least and most miserable of all will still be his brother. His love as shepherd of Israel claims to be in solidarity with the whole of human misery in all its ranges and ultimate depths: the Son of Man has come to seek and save that which was lost (Luke 19.10).[1]

We have just coined and used the perhaps somewhat paradoxical expression of juridical mysticism. One may wonder whether this theme of the Son of Man who is in sympathy and solidarity with all who are wretched can be called juridical. Catholic exegesis— that of Mersch for example—rightly finds in this text the theme of the Body of Christ; but it neglects the juridical and eschatological framework of the scene. Now it is essential to appreciate especially if we want to find the source and the exact meaning of the Pauline mysticism of life in Christ and of the

---

[1] Let us not forget that the image of the shepherd inspecting and dividing his flock had in Ezek. 34 a very precise sense: God will judge the strong who oppress or neglect the weak and will care for the weak sheep, the poor and the wretched who are defenceless in this world. The saying of Luke 19.10 proves that Jesus— Son of Man—wished to be this divine shepherd who comes to seek and save the lost. Jesus was certainly thinking of Ezek. 34.16: I will seek out that which was lost, I will bring back that which had gone astray. Without echoing every tone of the theme of the shepherd and the flock which in Ezek. 34 is amplified in every way, Jesus freely made use of it on several occasions, Matt. 9.36, 10.6, 18.10-14; Luke 15.4-7; John 10. The Ethiopian Apocalypse of Enoch also develops at length the allegory of the flock and the shepherd. Always both in the Jewish texts and with Jesus it is a question of the gathering together of Israel at the end of the age— of the Church.

Body of Christ, that the background here is justification and eschatology.

First of all let us not forget that the Being who reveals his mystery is the Son of Man, the Judge in an absolute sense; that we are present at a judgment, the only judgment which truly deserves this name. Around the Son of Man are his angels and his servants, who in Jewish thought are either accusers or defenders. And the men of all nations are going to be either condemned or declared just. In short we are confronted by the juridical and eschatological framework of the great debate between God and rebellious humanity. Let us note at once that this juridical and eschatological setting is alien to the myth of the *anthropos* such as we find it in oriental and gnostic syncretism. It is especially this setting which radically differentiates from the oriental and gnostic idea of the *anthropos* and the mystical body, the Jewish and Christian figure of the Son of Man and the Body of his Church. The difference can be summed up very briefly: in the gnostic myth, Man is the divine principle substantially and eternally identical with the sum of the souls of men scattered but predetermined to salvation.[1] In the thought of Jesus the Son of Man freely identifies himself with each of the wretched ones by an act of substitution and identification, and he will gather them together at the last day. Once again it is essential that the Son of Man, that is, Man, is not identified with humanity as a whole—Jesus is unfamiliar with this Stoic concept—but with each man. Thus it is not at all a question of an identity of substance between the primal man and the totality of his scattered members but of a sovereign act of self-identification. So soon as this distinction is not understood in its strictness—and it will be only too rarely understood in later tradition[2]—it means that we are certain to

[1] Not predestined but predetermined: myth knows neither a truly personal God nor a real history; it would be wrong to use the same term for two things which are so different.

[2] Consider for example the idea of the incarnation and the Body of Christ in Athanasius. The recent work of L. Bouyer on *L'Incarnation et l'Église-Corps du Christ dans la theologie de Saint Athanase*, Paris, *Unam Sanctam* 11, 1943, only confirms that this father of the Church, otherwise so remarkable, has curiously neglected justification by the Cross and developed a theory of redemption centring on the incarnation of the divine nature in human nature. Because he is obsessed by the Hellenistic problem of the divinization of human nature Athanasius arrives at a somewhat vitalist idea of redemption and the Body of Christ, at an equivocal synthesis between the biblical idea and the gnostic idea of the *anthropos* and his body.

misunderstand or to distort the meaning of the Christian mystical idea of the Body of Christ.

To indicate more precisely in what this juridical mysticism of the Son of Man consists, we must here say something in parenthesis. When we speak of the juridical element in the New Testament, we usually think only of the Pauline theory of justification, and even that theory has been singularly narrowed down; it has been reduced in practice to its individual aspect, its subjective effects: to the justification of the sinner before God. This limitation could not be imputed to the Reformers themselves, but Protestant theology received a one-sided expression in the question put by the monk of Erfurt: 'How can I have a merciful God, how can I be justified?' Nor will the development of recent centuries towards an increasingly subjectivist thought and piety facilitate the return to a more biblical and a wider vision. For when theology no longer takes really seriously the biblical statement that Satan is the accuser of men before God and their adversary on the earth we cannot but have a very limited idea of justification. To have some idea of the quite other dimensions of the concept of justification in the New Testament it suffices to read I Tim. 3.16, where, in a fragment of a hymn and confession which is doubtless very ancient, Christ is said to be justified by the Spirit. The Spirit by the resurrection of Jesus justifies before the tribunal of the world him who has just been condemned. When at his trial Jesus declares to his judges that they will see the Son of Man sitting at the right hand of God and coming with the clouds of heaven, and in effect says to them, another trial is taking place before God where I am the Judge and you are the accused; when Stephen, condemned like his Master, sees the heavens opened and the Son of Man standing at the right hand of God, they know that they are justified by and in the presence of God at the very moment when the justice of men condemns them to death. The difference between the two scenes which we have just alluded to, is that in the words of Jesus before the Sanhedrin, the Son of Man is seated, as Judge, while in the vision of Stephen he is standing as a witness to witness before God on behalf of his earthly witness, condemned like himself by the leaders of Israel. In both texts the Son of Man plays a part of capital importance in the celestial trial. He can be and he is both Judge and Witness. And as witness he can be according to Jewish law either *kategor* or *paraclet*, accuser or defender. In Rom. 8, that chapter which is central for the whole doctrine of justification, the Apostle Paul too opens a window through which we can catch a glimpse of the heavenly tribunal (Rom. 8.29-35): 'For whom he foreknew, he also foreordained to be conformed to the image of his Son, that he might be the first-born among many brethren: and whom he foreordained, them he also called: and whom he called, them he also justified: and whom he justified, them he also glorified. What then shall we say to these things? If God is for us, who is against us? He that spared not his own Son, but delivered him up for us all, how shall he not also with him freely give us all things? Who shall lay anything to the charge of God's elect? It is God that justifieth; who is he that shall condemn? It is Christ Jesus that died, yea rather, that was raised from the dead, who is at the right hand of God, who also maketh intercession for us. Who shall separate us from the love of Christ? . . .'

In this heavenly trial scene one character is missing: he whose name denotes accuser, Satan. It is very probable that Paul thinks like Jesus (Luke 10.18; John 12.31; cf. Rev. 12.10-22) that Satan, the prince of this world, has been cast out and replaced by the Paraclete, the intercessor. The angelic powers alone could still come into play; but they are subject to Christ. The juridical term Paraclete does not occur in Paul's writings: but the fact is there. nor does Jesus use it in Matt. 25.31-46: nevertheless the Son of Man fulfils not only the function of Judge but also that of witness-Paraclete on behalf of the elect and witness-accuser of the reprobate.

But let us return from this juridical setting to the heart of our text and try to characterize this juridical mysticism. Most exegetes talk as if Jesus had said in a somewhat rhetorical phrase: 'What you have done to the least of my brethren it is as if you had done it to me.' And it is left to the medieval rustic or to charming Christmas stories to take the text literally. Perhaps it will be objected that in Mark 9.37, Jesus says only 'He who receives one of these children *in my name* receives me', and that there is hardly any reason to see there anything more than the famous principle of rabbinic law mentioned above. But in the New Testament as a whole 'in my name' must be taken in a deep sense. In Mark 9.37, as elsewhere, the expression 'in the name of', current in the system of monetary exchange which obtained in antiquity, might lead us to suppose that Jesus was thinking only of a sort of heavenly substitution whereby acts of love towards a child are taken as done towards Jesus and God himself. And no doubt Jesus did think of a juridical manipulation of this sort. But in Matt. 25, and no doubt also in Mark 9.37, it is not only in the heavenly registers by ascribing as done to himself the least gesture of love made to the most wretched, but in reality, in flesh and blood, that the Son of Man has taken the place of his brothers, to identify himself unreservedly with their destiny. It is of course a question of a juridical substitution but it is also an effectual reality which goes as far as identification. Once again, what authorizes us to subtract anything at all from the formal and solemn declaration of the Son of Man? We must conclude that this Man has so become man that he has mysteriously but effectively taken and made his own the situation and destiny of each individual man. In this Jesus is saying as much as and more than John 1.14, 'and the Word became flesh'. He uses neither the term *logos* nor the term flesh. But he understands a substitution which massively includes what the Church will later call 'incarnation'. Further, he suggests that no moral act has value in itself: it has ultimate value only because mysteriously it reaches the Son of Man himself. Wonderfully sovereign claim of an absolute King, claim which ruins any idea that there is a good in itself, an abstract justice existing outside him, but which gives infinite value and divine glory to the humblest expression of love! The least service—and it is a question of small prosaic services of uncertain success: it is not said that the sick were cured, the prisoners were liberated—has relevance for the Son of Man, for God himself. And similarly, of course, the smallest omission takes on infinite gravity . . .

But on the other hand this Son of Man wished nothing for himself: with a no less sovereign authority he wishes only to have been served in the brethren.[1] Is there not here as it were

---

[1] Luther has written somewhere these admirable words: *Tu ama Deum in creaturis; non vult ut eum ames in majestate.*

an echo of Mark 10.45: 'For verily the Son of Man came not to be ministered unto but to minister, and to give his life a ransom for many'? And what is the meaning of Matt. 25, if not a mysterious substitution which resembles strangely that of Mark 10.45?

It is in this last judgment scene, perhaps, that the mystery of the Son of Man and of the person of Jesus is revealed to us both in its greatest profundity and in its grandiose wonderful simplicity. Jesus declares himself to be Son of Man and Judge, glorious King, the colossal figure of the apocalypses, the Byzantine 'Pantokrator', the Judge carved on the cathedral doorways of the middle ages, but he reveals that in this world he will have been mysteriously present in the most degraded wretch.

No finer commentary on this scene could be found than that contained in these verses of II Cor. 5.14, 21: 'For the love of Christ constraineth us; because we thus judge, that one died for all, therefore all died. And he died for all, that they which live should no longer live unto themselves, but unto him who for their sakes died and rose again. Wherefore we henceforth know no man after the flesh: even though we have known Christ after the flesh, we now know him so no more. Wherefore if any man is in Christ, he is a new creature: the old things are passed away; behold they are become new. . . .'

Behind each man the apostle sees the image of him who died and rose again for all, in whom this mysterious exchange has taken place. 'He who knew no sin was made sin for us, so that we should become the righteousness of God in him.' Hence the only reality which counts is this new life with Christ and in Christ: 'I am crucified with Christ. No longer I live; Christ liveth in me. The life I live at present in the flesh I live by faith in the Son of God who loved me and gave himself for me' (Gal. 2.20).

These texts of the apostle and all those which might be further cited show clearly enough that the Pauline mysticism has but amplified and pushed to its extreme consequences what Jesus had already indicated. The only difference is that the apostle writes after the death and resurrection of Jesus, while Jesus gives us the mysticism of the Son of Man in the terms in which it could be understood during his lifetime. Most of the differences of content between the thought of Jesus and that of Paul can be referred moreover to this difference of situation. The false differences, which liberal criticism has so much emphasized and which present-day critics happily tend to reduce, spring in large measure from a serious optical error of the moderns: instead of being viewed in their temporal succession, the teaching of Jesus and that of Paul have been juxtaposed and compared spatially. As though either of these teachings were a body of non-temporal truths about God. In fact they aim only at being commentaries on the events of the end. And this commentary could not be the same before and after the decisive event—the death and the resurrection of the Son of Man. May we be forgiven this truism, which is apparently forgotten: Jesus lived and taught before dying. The criticism made of Paul by the liberal school is like reproaching Shakespeare with not having made Lady Macbeth repeat in the third act the words which she spoke in the first. When, in short, will it be realized that Christian truths have a character which is more dramatic and temporal than Platonic and timeless?

Essentially everything is already implied in our text:

(*a*) The mystery of the Son of Man, both heavenly man and earthly man, identified with the most wretched. And this mystery, much more far-reaching than the 'Messianic secret', is prolonged in the life of every man.

(*b*) The mystery whereby the Son of Man is substituted for and identified with the elect people, the Israel of the end, for their justification.

(*c*) The mystery of the *body* of the new Man of which men have become members. In each of the members the head is present. If no distinction is here made between the Church and the new humanity which is the body of the *anthropos* the reason is that we are at the end of the age, when the two can no longer be distinguished.

(*d*) The source and the foundation of the Christian ethic: henceforth we must see every man and even ourselves no more after the flesh, but in the Son of Man or, as the apostle was to say very logically after the resurrection and exaltation of the Son of Man who had become King and Christ—'in Christ'.

One of the finest illustrations of our text is without a doubt to be seen in the following letter by which a citizen of Dortmund in 1369 founded a *hospitale pauperum*: 'As it seemed to me that it would be the summit of Christian perfection *Christum in suis membris quotidie visitare*, and gently and humbly to care for them in their misery, I have decided to convert my house into a hospital, *in quo Christus laudabiliter in suis membris honoraretur*.'[1]

Why after all did Jesus conjure up this last judgment scene? The sobriety of its style alone would prove that the purpose was not to give apocalyptic revelations. Quite on the contrary, as in all his evocations of the world to come Jesus energetically diverts the attention of his hearers from all indulgence in fanciful reverie about the future and inexorably brings them back to the present moment. The radical difference between Jewish apocalyptic and the eschatology of Jesus emerges here with perfect clarity. As in the majority of his parables Jesus returns again and again to this central theme: it is the present moment in its apparent banality which is decisive. This moment becomes invested with infinite seriousness not only because the time is short and the Parousia is near but because it is loaded with the infinite weight of the mysterious presence in our neighbour of the Son of Man and of God himself. Thus three new points arise which cannot be too much emphasized.

First, because man is confronted by his heavenly judge whenever he sees the need of his neighbour, the judgment and the final destiny of each one is in reality decided at the present moment. What the Johannine Christ will say about present judgment in the face of the Son and his Word will not go beyond what the Jesus of the Synoptics says here, and will only be somewhat more explicit. For this reason time is no longer an indifferent factor, it is deeply qualified by the secret and sovereign presence of him who is the master of time as of eternity. It may be said that time has now a deep radiating reality only in so far as it is Christo-centric. If we might modify the formula of the apostle we could say: now we no longer know time after the flesh. . . . The only moments which henceforth have positive value and are really historical are those which are filled with humble gestures of love and service. For such moments are already secretly pregnant with eternity.

[1] Quoted by W. Brandt, *op. cit.*

Then the idea of one's neighbour and the summary of the law are seen to have no longer their meaning in themselves; they must be viewed in a strictly Christo-centric light. The two commandments, 'Love God . . . Love thy neighbour . . .' are linked by a tie which is not merely rhetorical or simply a declaration of equivalence. They are linked and identified in depth through the mystery of the divine and human Son of Man, apart from whom, whether we realize it or not, we can love neither God nor neighbour. Finally, a last consequence is implied in this mystery: Jesus does not know man in himself as an abstraction. He knows only humanity his brothers. This implies the radical negation of all abstract humanism whether it be Stoic or modern. But on the other hand it means the affirmation of a humanism which is at once both sharply pointed and infinitely vast in extension, of a humanism which is rooted in the Man,[1] in him who might have said with far deeper meaning than the ancient sage understood by the words, *Homo sum: humani nihil a me alienum puto.*

[1] A detailed study of the Epistles to the Colossians and Ephesians would show how this mystery of the Man is there developed and explained in the most varied senses with an extraordinary richness. The style of these epistles is to a large extent that of the gnostic myth of the *anthropos* (cf. in particular Heinrich Schlier, *Christus und die Kirche im Epheserbrief*, Tübingen, 1930). But the thought is that of Jesus.

IV

THE VISION OF HISTORY IN THE NEW TESTAMENT[1]

CAN we speak of one vision, of a single conception of history in the New Testament? Are there not several, or rather several different attempts to suggest a philosophy of history? Do the Book of Revelation, Paul, John, and the Synoptics speak with one voice? These various witnesses are in fact somewhat divergent and limited as to their imagery and mode of thought. And this is due to three reasons:

(a) Biblical revelation is always concrete, and emerges within the context of human data relevant to a precise time and space; it is always incarnate.

(b) The biblical authors like ourselves walk by faith and not by sight.

(c) Above all the full and true meaning of history will be visible only at the last judgment. Human wretchedness and also the latent strength of a faithful theology will consist in being only a respectful and humble *theologia viatorum*. Any systematic philosophy of history leaving no room for mystery is excluded, as is also any type of facile providentialism: our God is not the God of the deists but the God of the Crucified; even the Son does not know the day and time of the Parousia.

And yet in the New Testament there is a real and deep unity, a single all-embracing vision of the chief focal points of history. Moreover the *Credo* very soon fixed like so many pegs a series of some few facts and it is one reason of its greatness that it only aimed at being a list of temporal events given without any abstract definition. Thus if there is no Christian philosophy of history there is a message concerning past, present and future history which is precise enough to demand and occasion our decision and to illuminate our faith.

We moderns, even—and perhaps especially—if we are Christians, experience, however, great difficulty in properly appre-

[1] Study presented to the Conference de Bossey (1949) and first published in the Review *Le Semeur*, 1950, Nos. 3-4, pp. 159-176.

hending the vision of history implicit in the Bible. We have it in our blood, in our retina, but in a distorted, impoverished and secularized form. We are in a sense bored and inoculated against it. We can neither accept nor reject it whole-heartedly. We have dropped, for example, a good part of the biblical hope; others have picked it up and we now receive it as a slap in our faces from the hands of the Marxists. Even the theologians have the *naïveté* to want to go on gathering apples after having conscientiously hewn down the trunk of the apple-tree: Christian ethics and the small change of Christian hopefulness cast into the world, yes! But we did not want to have anything more to do with the too naïve biblical conception of time and history. We have preferred the idea—and how grotesque it is—that history would secrete its own significance like an enormous endocrine gland.

It is not for me here to show how the apples have grown on the tree and have fallen: the dignity of man, king of creation, the possibility of a future greater than the past, of a science and technics dominating matter in the service of humanity, reason being no longer a ladder of escape towards immortality but an instrument to civilize a nature freed from the gloomy pagan deities, the new dignity of manual work, the possibility of social change since in principle every social system is superseded, the unity of the human race assured by a unified history whose meaning transcends itself, an ever-active love which does not give up even when confronted by the most desperate case—we have thought it possible to keep and develop all that by the light and heat we generate ourselves. And behold, all that has rotted in our hands. And the idea of history in particular. Like all Christian truths when isolated from their context this idea has run mad. Nietzsche saw clearly into the heart of the matter: to root out Christianity it is necessary to return to the cyclical notion of the Greeks. But it cannot be done. Even Sartre cannot resign himself to this, and history seems to remain for him a pathetic dialogue between man and the absence of God. One is not an atheist so easily. Reinold Niebuhr has observed that no one can return from a culture implying a sense of history to a culture which equates history with nature.[1]

[1] 'Faith and History' in *Theology Today*, April 1949, p. 37.

Let us try to return to the Bible: more pessimistic than all our pessimists, more optimistic than all our optimists, it can destroy all our optimistic and pessimistic illusions.

I. HISTORY NON-CYCLICAL

One commonplace but all-important fact dominates our problem: apart from certain Parsee tendencies and the religion of Israel, all the known metaphysical systems imply or profess a cyclical vision of time. History is only an aspect of the seasonal becoming of the forces of nature. By thus naturalizing history it is reduced to being an image of the mythologizing tendency. For cycle and myth are inseparable. Even with a Thucydides the myth dominates and naturalizes history: the task of the historian is to infer the general and non-temporal laws of cyclical becoming.

In the Bible, on the other hand, history transcends nature, time, space. The future will be richer than the past.

Nature itself is integral to the historical drama which takes place between man and God. It is subject to vanity and death on account of man, and it will be freed with the redemption of the sons of God. This means:

(*a*) That man, along with God whose image he is, is greater than the whole of nature. Christian humanism in principle secures to man a position superior to that which Prometheus sought (Ps. 8). Yet it is not a question of making time absolute. Above time there is God.

(*b*) This implies further that the Creator and the Redeemer God are one and the same. God does not create nature and then set history in motion; the first pages of Genesis—and criticism realizes this very clearly today—aim less at giving a cosmology than at marking the beginning of history. This account is primarily eschatological and sets the scene, in view of the drama which is about to be enacted between God and men. Besides, it is in the historical event of the exodus from Egypt that the nomad tribes received the revelation of Yahweh. Only subsequently did Israel realize that this Yahweh is the absolute Lord, hence also the creator of the cosmos. He is a Saviour, a living God, but completely free with regard to his people and the world. That also is why he creates the world *ex nihilo*, gratuitously: here there is no trace of oriental theogonies where Chronos engenders his children and then devours them. He is and will be every morning the Creator God: the world subsists, Israel and the nations live, only by his hand. Creation is grace and all grace is creation: 'May this world pass away, may grace come,' was the prayer of the primitive Church. The Kingdom of God is grace. Hence this history is unique in the annals of humanity: it glorifies no human greatness. The sins of Israel and of its leaders are by no means blurred. Mythical legend is in principle eliminated. Certainly there are legendary elements in the Old Testament as in the New. But this legend, if the term must be used, is in reverse. Instead of idealizing and glorifying men it puts them in their place. If the nativity stories are legendary, which is possible, they are typical; they glorify in reverse by emphasizing the lowly wretched character of the origins of Jesus. *In the Bible there is no mythologizing of history but on the contrary a historicizing of mythical elements.* Non-temporal mythological legend disembodies events. Biblical legend temporalizes, historicizes, incarnates. It glorifies not man but God.

2. HISTORY AND MYTH[1]

In breaking the cycle of oriental myths biblical thought shatters myths in general.[2] It subjugates and freely exploits the fragments of myths which are to be found in its baggage of materials, images and concepts. This may be seen on every page of the Old Testament, and equally in the New. In the latter the oriental myth of the anthropos is used in the service of the doctrine of the true Adam. Paul explodes the myth of the primitive Man by saying that the second and the true Adam is infinitely superior to the first. The struggle of the authors of the New Testament against gnostic mythology shows us with striking clarity that *the redemption realized in the course of the history of salvation is much more than the restoration of the paradisiacal state: it is a new creation which, while fulfilling, far transcends the first.* Although the memories of a paradisiacal state serve in the New Testament as

[1] Cf. O. Cullmann, *Christ et le Temps*, pp. 66-74.
[2] 'Circuitus illi jam exposi sunt' (Augustine, *De civitate Dei*, I, 12, 20, 4).

in the Old to substantiate the hope of a future good time, they are not essential. Further they were by their very nature orientated more towards the future than towards the past.

Biblical anthropology borrows from Genesis only a cursory survey. *Its substance is taken rather from the history of salvation. Man is that historic being whose life is rooted in his encounter with God.* Whereas in gnostic systems the myth of the anthropos determines and modifies Christology, in the New Testament and especially in Paul it is Christology which dominates anthropology. As well in the Sermon on the Mount as in the Epistles it is Jesus Christ who is the new and true man.

We have not paid sufficient attention to the important fact noted by Max Weber that we never find in the Old Testament the idea that Yahweh might be, like the gods of Hinduism, for example, the metaphysical guarantor of a hierarchy of castes, of an immutable social order. Neither cyclic myth nor static ethics but history. In social ethics this point is of capital importance and relativizes, for example, every static theory of natural rights.

Fierce discussion is going on about the necessity of demythologizing the biblical message in order to translate it into the framework of modern concepts. Bultmann[1] does so and to some extent Dodd[2]: they have this in common, that they wish to relegate to the periphery of the New Testament message the myth of the Parousia. I think that here there is a theological and historical error. Two facts seem to me essential:

(*a*) Ancient cosmology was not radically modified, in its spatial aspect, by the Bible: for example the story of the flood conforms on the whole with Babylonian cosmology. On the other hand this cosmology has been fundamentally changed in its *temporal* aspect. Let us then demythologize the spatial ideas: the above, the below, the seven heavens, the underworld . . . but we must be careful not to touch the temporal framework. In ignoring this essential distinction Bultmann lapses into a sort of existentialist gnosis where history loses its meaning except in its reduced anthropological terms, while C. H. Dodd dissolves eschatology

---

[1] R. Bultmann, *Neues Testament und Mythologie*, republished in *Kerygma und Mythos*, Hamburg, 1948. (E.T. *Kerygma and Myth*, 1954.)
[2] C. H. Dodd, *The Parables of the Kingdom*, 1935; *History and the Gospel*, 1948.

in a sort of Platonizing idealism; D-day would really have been enough for the first Christians, the V-day of the Parousia and of the new creation would be only a myth symbolizing God's mastery of all the periods of history.

(*b*) Because of the disparity between past and future a difference should be marked between the mythical elements which concern the origins and those which concern the end of history. The former aim less at explaining the 'how' of the beginning than the 'why', the *telos* of history. Thus theology must and can accept the most solid results of geology and pre-history. But it will be very realistic in maintaining the concrete and temporal character of the coming of the Kingdom of God, of the Parousia of the new creation, the new heavens, and the new earth.

3. ALL THEOLOGY IS HISTORY

That writing of the New Testament which is apparently the most speculative, the Epistle to the Hebrews, is also the one which stresses with the maximum force the fact that Christians *are but pilgrims on the way towards the goal of history* (Heb. 11-12): *Historia viatorum, non angelorum.* Christian theology is no non-temporal philosophy or ethic. It is essentially *a commentary*, a reminder, an interpretation and declaration of a series of events of an *oikonomia*, an *ordo salutis*. It is hardly concerned with truth in itself, in the theoretical sense. The web of reality and truth consists of a dialogue between persons, between God and men, a vast conflict between light and darkness where each act and each scene have their precise, unique and necessary place. This drama takes place on the earth in our time and space and not in the oneness of time, the a-chronism of myth. When the times were fulfilled God sent forth his Son (Gal. 4.4). The eternal Word became flesh under Augustus, died under Tiberius, and the brutal Pontius Pilate has found his place in the *Credo*. To know God and have life it is necessary to eat the flesh and drink the blood of the Son of Man, to accept the folly and scandal of the incarnation, and lamentable death of Jesus of Nazareth in all its obscure commonplaceness. And yet the flesh profiteth nothing. It is the Spirit which giveth life. Although the Logos was clothed with historical reality the real is not, as Hegel would have it, immediately logical. That is true not only of the origins and end of history, which are essentially beyond the ken of man, but also of the events in the history of salvation which lie within our purview. To recognize in the healing miracles of Jesus something other than the exploits of a magician, they must be viewed in a certain light; to see in the incidental fact of a certain gallows raised in the year 29 the centre of history, we must be enlightened from above. The events of the revelation remain ambivalent signs; the revelation is largely incognito. Some few only have seen and touched the Risen Lord; blessed are those who have not seen and yet have believed. This whole history is clear and continuous only for faith. Of course the Gospel is simple, it is not at all complicated. But it is difficult.

This does not mean that in order to organize the brute material, the raw facts, of the story of salvation we must cast over it a network of forms, categories and general ideas. It is not ideas, it is the Spirit which giveth life, that is, the living God who is Spirit, the living and personal God who sheds the light of faith on man. The way in which John sees and writes history is in this respect characteristic. His faithfulness is different from that of a legal witness; a legal witness or a documentary film would not have been faithful to Jesus. *What is real is our history with God and our neighbour.* History is neither a web of horizontal human decisions and determinism nor a purely vertical affair enacted between God and a few mystical souls. It is a drama both simple and complex taking place between God and his creatures. And this drama has a centre which is also its origin and end.

4. CHRIST, THE CENTRE OF HISTORY

When we pass from Jewish apocalypses to the Gospels we are conscious of a global impression: that of an extraordinary concentration.

First in the sphere of concepts: Jewish thought moved particularly around two ideas stemming in part from Iran, of the present and evil aeon and the future and glorious aeon. Jesus puts in the centre an expression which in Jewish writings is not frequent: that of the Kingdom of God. Jesus is radically theocentric. While maintaining the vigorous dualism of the apocalypses, he surpassed it, for he develops the line of Old Testament thought into this fundamental certainty: *God reigns and he will reign.* What is more, this reign has drawn near, it has come upon you, it is at work in the midst of you (Luke 17.20). Jesus focusses his attention no longer upon a more or less problematic and distant future but upon the present instant, which acquires a unique and gravity; this present instant is decisive (Matt. 25.31). While using the outline material and the palette of Jewish apocalyptic Jesus concentrates and simplifies in the extreme his pictures of the future. For anyone who has read Enoch and Baruch the sobriety of his words is most striking: they are fraught with a sovereign intimacy and an infinite reverence for the mystery of the divine Kingdom.

But this concentration goes much further: *the Kingdom of God is at work not in general but at a precise point, in a person, in Jesus, in his words and sovereign deeds.* To those outside Jesus speaks especially of the Kingdom of God; to his intimate friends he will speak in particular of the Son of Man. *As divine Man and true Adam he is engaged in reversing the whole course of the history of Adam.* He has conquered Satan in the desert; he has bound the strong man and is beginning to pillage his domain. By his healing miracles, by stilling the storm and raising the dead, he stands forth as King of creation. When he says 'But I say unto you . . .' he places himself above Moses as the Lord of the Torah, who is both fulfilling and transcending all that the ancient covenant promised. A greater than Solomon is here: the wisdom of God embodied in a Person; more than Jonah: here is the true prophet who has been speaking in all previous prophets. He can forgive sins, a privilege which belongs only to God. *In a word, in him the new world of the resurrection makes an irruption into the old.*

But the time of triumph has hardly dawned. These victories are as yet only signs. This Son of Man must first serve as the servant of the Eternal and suffer and die as a ransom for all. He can do so for he is true Man in the image of God and has become incarnate as all men, in him is concentrated the remnant of faithful humanity and of Israel. From Adam to the coming of the Kingdom of God one can discern in the Bible a single line leading to the death and resurrection of the Christ. Man was from the first the representative of the whole creation before God; his revolt involves him in death. After Adam and Noah God elects a people in Abraham, an obscure tribe drawn from a remote corner of history. Rosenberg was right: the Jewish problem is certainly the key to the history of the world. This elect and blessed people multiplies, but its revolt brings about an ever-increasing reduction: only a remnant of Israel will subsist in place of the people. And now this remnant is reduced to a single man who alone is the Son of Man.[1] His death for the people and for all peoples opens up a movement of liberation in the universe. Those who believe in him are members of the body of the new Adam. And this body is in principle aimed at the inclusion of all men. Thus in the Bible there is neither static particularism nor static universalism but a sort of universalist concentration and expansion. In Christ all are *one* and all are sons of Abraham (Gal. 3.28). Through the final revelation of the sons of God biological creation itself, groaning for its deliverance, will at last enjoy its flowering.

That in part explains the theological importance of the destruction of Jerusalem in 70. Since the true temple is henceforth the Christ and his Body made of living stones, the old world can begin to disappear. The destruction of the Holy City is the sign of the end of this old world and the coming of the new world. Judgment begins, in history, with the house of God.

By virtue of his total obedience to the Father Jesus breaks the reign of Satan the Accuser, who accused men day and night before God (Rev. 12.10; John 12, 31; Luke 10.18), and takes his place as Paraclete, Defender, and Intercessor for all men. By the mystery of a juridical but objective substitution, he has made his own the destiny and the sin of each man. Henceforth he stands behind the most wretched of men. 'I was naked and ye clothed me. . . .' The private and most lowly story of the most insignificant of men is assumed and transfigured by this Son of Man. And every man, confronted by his neighbour, stands truly face to face with the Son of Man, with God himself. For this crucified and risen Son of Man has been raised to the right hand of God

[1] Cf. T. W. Manson, *The Teaching of Jesus*; O. Cullmann, *op. cit.*, pp. 81-82.

where he secretly reigns until he shall visibly reign in the sight of all. He reigns not only over the elect but in principle and already in fact over all men and all powers which are at present in control of the world and its history.

But before explaining the implications of this reign of Christ we must briefly sketch the meaning of his sovereignty over past and future. The Prologue of John's Gospel, in a few simple words, explains that the eternal Word was at the beginning of creation, that the Son has always been the light and the life of men. All was created by him and for him. The history of the elect people and of all peoples gathers from him its origin, its end and its meaning. He was the Word which does not return void (Isa. 54.11), the fire, the hammer which breaketh in pieces the rock (Jer. 23.29) and makes history. Above all he will bring all things under his dominion: ἀνακεφαλαιώσασθαι (Eph. 1.10). Even the world of the dead is submitted to him. When he has put down his last enemy, death, he will commit the kingdom to the Father; and God will be all in all. He will reign with the Father over a new world where there will be but love, service, joy and adoration. Then will come a time which according to the profound word of the Apocalypse of Baruch will have no end. It will indeed be time, and also space, that are real, and there will be spiritual bodies more real than our poor reality of the present life. Let us not abandon to the Marxists the realistic pages of the Bible to delight ourselves only in the salvation of the soul. God is more materialistic than Marx, whom we would do better to reproach with his optimism about the goodness of post-revolutionary man; the new world will be truly a new creation still more real than the first. Only this realism is at the same time radically personalist. It is impossible to write a biology of eternal life or the geography and chronology of the Kingdom of God. The question which worried the apocalyptists: when will the reign of God come? and how? becomes secondary. The *telos* is no longer a future unknown term, it is a person who has been seen, heard and touched. Eschatology is concentrated in Christology. Eternal life is to know the Father in the Son. It is life and communion with them in concrete reality. Jesus does not merely give the bread of life, he is the bread of life.

5. THE TIME OF THE CHURCH

As practical men the first witnesses attach particular importance to the present period of history, the time of the Church. The present time between the resurrection and the Parousia is characterized by the paradox of a 'not yet' and a 'but already'. On the one hand the new world has already appeared in Christ in the global and unique event of his death and resurrection. In principle the general resurrection and the new creation should break forth without delay. That is why the disciples, faithful to the hope of the Jews and of John the Baptist who did not distinguish between the two comings of the Son of Man, and saw in the Baptism of Spirit and of fire the new creation springing forth as a whole, ask Jesus: 'Dost thou now set up the Kingdom of Israel?' Then Jesus tells them something extraordinary: the history of the world, essentially terminated, will continue with its ups and downs. Why? It is for God only to appoint times and hours, but you will receive the Holy Ghost and will be my witnesses in Jerusalem and to the ends of the earth. If history is prolonged the reason is that God wills to save Israel and the nations of the whole earth. The only reason for the continued existence of history is to enable the Gospel to reach the last of mankind. This Gospel will be proclaimed . . . then will come the end (Matt. 24.14). John can write, 'It is the last hour' (I John 2.18). The decisive event has taken place in Christ. The light shines already and this world passes away. The duration of this intermediate time matters little. Hence the New Testament shows no interest in apocalyptic chronological schemes, in time-tables of weeks = 6,000 cosmic years plus the millennium. It is sober because it has Jesus Christ. It is to misunderstand the Revelation to seek in it such a time-table and the five-year plan of God.

The gift of the Spirit gives to the faithful the assurance that the Kingdom of God is coming: it is the first fruits and the pledge of the life to come. A witness, it makes them witnesses and martyrs. It allows them to take their place in the history of salvation. From Adam to Christ they recognize that it is a question of their personal destiny. Dying with Adam they know that they are made alive in Christ. The deeper meaning of the Old

Testament is unveiled to them. There they read in the story of the Exodus a prophecy of the life of the Church (I Cor. 10.11). The Spirit recalls to them the words of Jesus and enlightens them. It makes present to them the event of the Christ. The future is assured to them and already pledged in the first fruits of the Spirit, which gives them a fervent and serene certitude that salvation approaches with every minute (Rom. 13.11). In the cult and the sacraments the Christian is in communion with every aspect of the history of salvation. In a word, the Christ raised to the right hand of God exercises his reign by the Spirit in the Church. Cullmann has shown that the earliest confessions in the Church, of which the most simple and the most central is the *Kyrios Christos*, affirm above all this living royalty of the Crucified. The old Aramaic hymn, quoted by Paul in Phil. 2.5-11, proclaims that every knee bends to Jesus in heaven, on earth and under the earth, and that every tongue confesses that he is the Lord. Thus the Church is open to the world. It aims at converting the whole world. In this period of the mission and of the Spirit in the Church, the latter has no other function than to be the instrument, the body of its living head, proclaiming before the world that he is its sole Lord. Thus all the powers of the cosmos and of history will be subjected to Christ. Are they already so or will they be so in the end? On this point the Bible gives a paradoxical answer. According to II Tim. 1.10, for example, victory is already won and actual, but I Cor. 15.25 and Heb. 10.13 place the total triumph in the future. In Rom. 8 the two assertions appear side by side.[1]

They may seem to us very strange, these angelic and demonic powers. Since the eighteenth century we have reduced the religious drama to two partners: God and man. With a superior smile we have eliminated the roles of Satan and his acolytes and also that of the angels of God and all this curious *cortège* of principalities and powers. Have we done well? Even the great psychologist Jung has just affirmed the objective existence of demonic forces. If evil exists beyond and above man it must indeed be an evil will, hence someone rather than something. When one no longer believes in the existence of Satan one inevitably satanizes one's opponents. After having been so stupid

[1] Cf. O. Cullmann, *op. cit.*, pp. 108 ff.

as to satanize Hitler we now satanize Stalin or capitalism. These powers of which the Bible speaks are not satanic but ambivalent. They are creatures which have received from God a cosmic and especially a historic mission. They like to think themselves autonomous and wise. The principalities of this aeon crucified the Lord (I Cor. 2.8): behind Caiphas and Pilate, Paul discerns these powers which control statesmen. In Judaism the nations had their angels (Dan. 12.1). The apostle says that all these authorities come from God (Rom. 13.1): in spite of the ambivalence of the state the Christian must serve it for the sake of justice. All these powers are in principle subjected not only to God but to Christ. They are not vaguely subordinate to the distant supervision of a general providence—this deistic view has been catastrophic in many ways—they are responsible before Christ. The states and all historic greatness are thus subject to the *Regnum Christi*. These forces which secular history calls powers, these movements and 'isms' which are far from being nominalistic abstractions, are personified by the Bible to show that they are responsible, that there are collective responsibilities, but also to emphasize that men are sometimes only their agents and victims. Above all, the Bible declares that none of these realities is ultimate. The Christian is freed from the elements of this world, from determinisms through which these powers seem to mock at him. He is made in the image of God in Christ, and not merely in the standard image of his environment. God himself mobilized Pilate to achieve salvation, and the Roman roads convey the Gospel. The *Pax Romana*, like persecution by the state regarded as the beast, can only have the effect of furthering the cause of the Gospel. Of course it is clear that all things have not yet been subjected to him (Heb. 2.8). The enormous beasts of Daniel, so inhuman, rise up and do battle from century to century; but in actual fact God 'has put all things under his feet and has made him supreme head of the Church' (Eph. 1.22). Satan has been cast out. If he still ravages the earth it is because he knows that his time is short (Rev. 12.12).

Thus the movement of evangelization which follows the death and the resurrection of Christ aims through the Church at the whole world. This slender stream of history formed by the elect people, by Jesus, and his twelve companions, pours out in a torrent into the great rivers of history. The head of the Church is also the head and the King of the cosmos (Col. 1.17). By his death he has reconciled all things to himself. He has received all power, and sends his own to baptize all nations. It is not said that besides the Church there will also be a *corpus christianum*. Knowing only the *Corpus Christi* the New Testament excludes all clericalism. But through the Church the dominions and powers learn the manifold and flexible wisdom of God (Eph. 3.10). And this wisdom reveals the mystery that one day all Israel, the Gentiles as well as the elect people, will enter into the new world (Rom. 11.25). *The Church must therefore proclaim the Gospel in its fulness not only to individuals but to states, to cultural, economic and other collective groups.*

6. THE HISTORY OF SALVATION AND SOCIAL ETHICS

This vast perspective, disclosing a movement of concentration followed by one of expansion, and springing from the life of the new Adam, allows us to understand a rather disturbing fact which introduces an extraordinary complication into the problem of Christian social ethics. It is well known that the New Testament is somewhat poor in regard to precise directives concerning the social and political message which the Church should bring to the world. The prophets are in this respect much richer. This insular concentration on the problems arising out of the life of Christians among themselves, this limitation of the horizon, is it ultimate or provisional with the early Christians? Is it not rather a matter of necessary potentiality?

The attitude towards the pagan state, for example, seems to reduce itself to an attitude of passive obedience limited by obedience towards God, and to fail to recognize the importance of public prophetic criticism and of initiatives for the amelioration of the social structure. This limitation is due in part to the facts of the situation: Jesus lives and speaks within the limits of Palestine, the authors of the Epistles address themselves to small scattered groups without social or political importance. But it is also due to a special situation in the process of salvation. During his lifetime Jesus had formally forbidden his envoys to preach to the heathen. He gives it to be understood by the Greeks who come to see him that his death alone will enable all men to be drawn unto Him (John 12.32). The prayer of Jesus for the world will be strangely concentrated on this small handful of men by whom he wishes to convert it (John 17). Hence the Church has primarily a missionary task and ethic. Moreover any outward change in the social structure would only result in another legalistic system.

Since Jesus himself is the true Law, all ethical life can only be life in Christ. He is himself the living Way, the true norm of conduct. He is at work in this old world through his Body the Church. 'It shall not be so among you' (Mark 10.43). At first sight the social doctrine of the New Testament seems patriarchal and conservative. But essentially any idea of a static unchanging social hierarchy is irrelevant. 'The fashion of this world passeth away' (I Cor. 7.31). In the Church, the Body of the new Adam, all barriers of race and class are broken down. This mystery of the new man of Ephesians, Colossians and Romans 9-11, cannot help but translate itself into the social structure to some extent. The life of this body as suggested in Rom. 12 and I Cor. 12 cannot but radiate into the surrounding world and produce sooner or later an echo, a reflection, an analogy relative but real in the life of the city. The poor will be the object of a new attention and respect; the great will descend from their pedestal. The New Testament does not profess democracy; but in saying in I Peter 2.17: 'Honour all men . . . fear God, honour the king', it gives the king his status as a man who has received from God a special function. The political régime nearest the Gospel will tend towards an organism of mutual responsibilities and controls. Again, the institution of slavery, as is known, is not condemned in the New Testament, but it is made void from within. Where men live with their slaves as Paul with Onesimus, their living dignity as men cannot but in the long run annul a status which has become merely formal. If Christ has conquered the powers and elements of the cosmos and the social and political worlds, the dualism between a religious and a supposedly irremovable patriarchal social order is no longer possible.

The witness of Christians will raise the sign of the victory of Christ in every sphere of life.

It would be a serious anachronism to apply directly the scattered indications of the New Testament as if they were a complete and non-temporal code of social ethics: it would mean reducing them to a mixture of conformism and passive abstentionism. The problem of the active and public transformation of the social structure is not raised in the New Testament because it could not be. These tiny groups had no possibility of action on a large scale. To attempt to imitate them by an ill-informed biblicism would be to fail to appreciate the fact that the difference between them and us is not merely historical but theological. Of course in a world which is still hostile to its Lord the Church remains and must remain above all a missionary church. But its missionary task has widened and deepened. Almost everywhere Christians can influence the public life of the surrounding world; they are sufficiently numerous; the technical resources of modern life have opened up possibilities of big social transformations. We are not asked to accept the myth of a 'Christian civilization' with its retinue of clericalism and crusade, but to believe that we can and must raise everywhere signs of the reality of the Body of the new Man. If we believe that the living Christ edifies and builds up his Body in our history, we can no longer regard any man or any situation according to the flesh, as ruled exclusively by the supposed autonomous and immutable powers of blood, economic laws, and politics: we regard every man in Christ (II Cor. 5.16). Further, our action should not be checked by the possibility of the sudden advent of the reign of God. This belief may have limited the horizon of the early Christians at one or two points; in fact it rather stimulated them to act more effectively and quickly so as to carry the Gospel everywhere. We who know that this imminence is qualitative rather than quantitative may not camouflage behind this hope our fear of bearing witness. In the distressed world of our atomic era the Church must adopt the serene, adventurous and encouraging attitude of the apostle which he reveals in the storm scene of Acts 27.

7. IS PROGRESS A FACT?

In our present situation between the old world, in essence defeated but still terribly aggressive, and the new world already real in Christ and at work by the Spirit in the Church and the world, must Christians mark time in an indecisive struggle or can they advance in quality and quantity? Of course history sees repeated the madness of man bringing about an almost infernal series of deterministic cycles but it sees also repeated the fidelity of God who prevents history from being nothing but gloomy repetitiveness. Jewish apocalyptic tended globally towards a rather pessimistic and restrictive vision. In the New Testament we find on the one hand Revelation, Matt. 24, and especially Luke 18.8: 'When the Son of Man cometh, shall he find faith on the earth?' And on the other hand Romans 9-11, Colossians and Ephesians, which suggest rather an extension of the Kingdom of Christ and a building up of his Body through history. Yet the apparently consistent argument of Ephesians includes also the terrible final struggle announced in Eph. 6. In short, the words of Jesus seem to suggest a sort of growth of the wheat and tares and a deepening of the conflict such as will culminate in the opposition of antichrist and Christ through a process of diabolic imitation. This very imitation is a confession of the defeat of Satan: he betrays his inferiority complex. It seems to me that in indicating these two directions, without seeking to harmonize them, the New Testament intends to put us on our guard against all theories, whether apocalyptic or evolutionist, against pessimistic or optimistic illusions, against the sectarian complex of the oppressed as against Roman or liberal clericalism, which believes that it is about to realize on earth the Kingdom of God by means of some philosophic or social system. It wishes to remind us that the future belongs to God and to God alone; that it conceals unexpected possibilities until the moment of final victory. What is certain is that God will give his Church both victory and suffering, and most often victory through defeat. The mortification of Jesus is in operation in it (II Cor. 4.10), but also the power of his resurrected life. The one and the other attest that the Christ continues to reign from the height of his Cross. Further, the Church remains a poor terribly human thing. Hence the deep ambivalence of the history of the Church and of every biography of a great Christian. In spite of considerable differences we see everywhere tares in the wheat. Hence in the truly Christian historian we find a certain relativism, a sense of the complexity of things and of men which will always preclude any facile providentialism, any apologetic and unctuous hagiography. For the history of the Church, like that of the world, is a strife in which man seeks constantly to justify himself, but God manifests in his anger and mercy that he alone is just. Any vision of the history of the Church which does not at every moment breathe the spirit of the *sola gratia*, the *semper peccator*, and the *semper poenitens* of Luther, is a monstrous negation of the Gospel. It is on the spiritual heights where rages the battle between the mystery of Satan, the mystery of the decision of man, and especially the mystery of God in Christ.

Hence between D-Day and V-Day, to use again the suggestive image of Cullmann, the sole strategy of the Church will consist in the leading of its invisible head. We can only be vigilant, i.e. ready for anything. Must we be ready to live tomorrow in the catacombs or must we be prepared for an evangelization of the masses, a world-wide Christian culture? I think that the Bible might remind people like Latourette that it is not so certain that the missionary movement will continue to be an advance through storm, and the people who think in terms of catastrophe that God may tomorrow fling wide to us immense gateways of advance. After all, may not the impossibility of discerning the outlines of any Christian philosophy of history be a secret and wonderful benediction? Do we really need one? Is it our faith or our lack of faith which wants to know what will happen? The Lamb alone has received and can unseal the book of the future (Rev. 5.1). We do not need to know precisely what we must think of the question of progress. It suffices us to know that because Christ is risen our labour, however obscure and desperate it may seem, is not in vain in the Lord (I Cor. 15.58). In our old, tired and weary Europe I should be personally inclined to think like Jeremiah. If I had money I would buy a field at the height of a siege; and would be inclined to a certain optimism.

It is possible that European civilization is in agony. That would be a pity but not at all a reason for despair. Projecting their systems into myths, pagan societies, Sisyphus-like, attempt to fixate time and to escape from it; but their finest myths open out only on to death. Shortly before Valéry it was discovered that all civilizations are mortal. One kingdom only will survive —that of God. By tracing for all human greatness a precise limit (Acts 17.26), the Bible checks the innate immoderation of man, and just in so doing confers on history a meaning. The Greeks were not wrong in thinking that for man the infinite is chaos, that the finite, the limited alone, is perfect. To be civilized is to dwell in a circumscribed city, to have a precise norm and place, an integral *politeia*. In the city which will embody the reign of God—which will not be a church but a very lay community—they will also bring the glory of the nations. Of what will it consist? It will probably consist of something very different from what we like to think is glorious.

CONCLUSION

For there is the last judgment. Is it because the Church of former days held out the threat of it too much that we neglect it? In any case it is strange that it figures so little in the theology and preaching of the Church. For many years, for example, Karl Barth has ceased to speak of it. Cullmann hardly mentions it. Niebuhr, like Barth of thirty years ago, seems to see only present judgment. There is certainly already a judgment implied in present events. The Magnificat proclaims that God abases the proud and exalts them of low degree. We should see in the storms of history the judgments of God foreshadowing the last judgment and in temporary deliverances the signs of the coming Kingdom. But there is also the last judgment which relativizes our poor human judgments and puts them in their place; it is above all our great consolation: one day the men and things of this world will be allocated to their true position, a new earth will at last know the meaning of justice.

It is only when we do not take seriously the last judgment that we feel obliged to settle accounts within history, to make a philosophy of history, to neglect the parable of the wheat and the tares, and to lapse into the dogma—so confused and superficial—'that history will judge'. The biblical vision neither denies nor diminishes at all the complexity of historical phenomena. Nor does it encase them in a system. It believes, without claiming to foresee it, that all things will ultimately contribute to the victory of God. God is free and man too can always decide for or against Christ and his neighbour. In the vision of the last

79

judgment (Matt. 25.31-46), the Son of Man seems to ignore, with a sovereign indifference to the grandeurs of history, what men consider to be great and lasting. He reveals on the other hand a passionate interest in each individual man, his obscure wretchedness, and his miserable lonely destiny. God and Christ incline their ear towards man in the concrete and in his private history. The sole criterion will be—You have served me or you have not served me in my brothers. The greatest glories and the vast swelling pomps of this world will burst like soap bubbles, the smallest act of love will be magnified with the dimension of Christ. The truly historic moments will be very different from those singled out by the historians. The end of the vast drama of history will be a total surprise for all, even for the elect.

Hence our final word about history will emphasize that it is above all *a mystery*. As a conclusion of that outline theology of history which is Romans 1-11, Saint Paul can only celebrate this mystery that (Rom. 11.25) through all the pagan idolatries and the hardening of Israel God has shut up all men in disobedience that He might have mercy on all.

'O the depth of the riches both of the wisdom and the knowledge of God! How unsearchable are his judgments and his ways past tracing out! For of him and through him and unto him are all things' (Rom. 11.33-36).

V

WAS THE LAST SUPPER A PASCHAL MEAL?[1]

ONE of the most complex problems set for the historian and theologian by the various Passion narratives is without a doubt that of the exact date of the death of Jesus.

It is well known that our accounts differ on a most important point: although they agree to place the death of Jesus on the Friday, the Gospel of John and the Synoptics state with unquestionable clarity, the former that Jesus died on the eve of the Jewish Passover, 14th Nisan, and the latter that he died the following day, 15th Nisan, during the afternoon of the feast day. These two traditions are irreconcilable.

This chronological point would hardly affect the content and meaning of the Gospel narratives and would have a mere chronological interest were it not that it is indissolubly bound up with the far more important problem of the true and original meaning of the last meal that Jesus took with his disciples.

If Mark, followed by Matthew and Luke is right, then this last meal was a Paschal meal. If John is right this meal could not have been a passover, but Jesus died a few hours before Israel ate the Paschal lamb.

We do not propose to review the many hypotheses which up to the present have been suggested to solve the problem. We will recall only that in spite of the marked preference which most critics accord to the Marcan tradition and the somewhat prejudiced distrust with which they examine the Johannine traditions, they mostly tend to follow John rather than Mark on this particular point of chronology. In fact the Marcan tradition is very difficult to reconcile with what we know of the Jewish laws and customs of the period. It is inconceivable that Jesus should have been judged, condemned and crucified in the midst of the feast. That would have been contrary to the most formal prescriptions of the law. It is impossible to understand, for example, why the disciples should be armed in Mark 14.47, and why Simon of Cyrene in Mark 15.21 should be returning from the fields at

[1] Appeared first in the *Theologische Zeitschrift* of Basle, 1948, No. 2, pp. 81-101.

noon at the height of the feast. But we can understand very well why he should return at noon on the eve of the Passover, for we know that it was permissible to work in the fields until noon on that day. This detail of the Marcan tradition thus rather strengthens the Johannine data. Further, the story of the last meal as given in Mark mentions neither the Paschal Lamb nor the unleavened bread. Only the main part of Luke's story tends more clearly, rightly or wrongly, by speaking of the two cups, to present the meal as a passover. Above all the Marcan tradition is not only difficult to reconcile with a series of facts in the narrative but it contradicts itself in formal terms: the verses Mark 14.1-2: 'Now after two days was the feast of the passover and the unleavened bread . . . not during the feast,' presupposes in fact, if the notice has any meaning, the chronology of John. And is it not significant that Luke has omitted this statement? He must have seen that it contradicts the chronology which he thought the correct one, and careful as usual to present a coherent narrative he could only disregard it.

Hence many critics have decided in favour of the Johannine chronology, which is coherent and does not set insoluble problems.[1] Yet there is a slight tendency to suspect the Johannine chronology, which seems governed by a theological motif: John seems to wish to insist that Jesus died as a real Paschal Lamb.

Other critics have attempted in various ways to harmonize the contradictory data of the Gospels. The ingenious theories of Chwolson, followed by Klausner and Lichtenstein, Strack, and above all, Billerbeck, postulate that the Pharisees and part of the people among whom was Jesus celebrated the Passover a day before the Sadducees—hence the difference between Mark and John. Attractive hypothesis, the only defect of which is that it is unsubstantiated.

Finally, certain authors have put forward the hypothesis that the last meal was a true Paschal meal, but was ante-dated by

[1] Joachim Jeremias, *Die Abendmahlsworte Jesu*, Göttingen, 1935, gives on pp. 10-12 a detailed list of the partisans of Mark, on pp. 12-14 that of the partisans of John. Among the first let us mention Jülicher, Zahn, Merx, Billerbeck, Dalman, W. Bauer, J. E. Carpenter, A. Schweitzer, Torrey, Schniewind. Among the second are Strauss, Renan, Goetz, Batiffol, J. Weiss, Wellhausen, Burkitt, Heitmüller, G. Beer, Loisy, Schlatter, Oesterley, Lietzmann, K. L. Schmidt, Bultmann, M. Dibelius. Finally Goguel and Bertram are altogether sceptical.

Jesus himself to the previous day.[1] Yet this theory is in conflict with various points in the narrative of Mark which are unfavourable to the idea of a Paschal meal—no mention of the lamb nor of unleavened bread—especially with the fact that such a private anticipation was impossible. Besides, it has no real basis in the texts.

The hypothesis which we would like to add to the dossier is both akin to the preceding one and also very different. There was certainly an anticipation not of the Paschal meal itself but of the Paschal motifs, and oral tradition has taken this meal for a true Paschal meal and thus given rise to the mistaken chronology of Mark. We shall try to show that this hypothesis has a real basis in the texts. Let us take as our point of departure this curious verse which Luke has inserted at the beginning of his story of the last meal, Luke 22.15: 'And he said to them, With desire I have desired to eat this passover with you before I suffer: for I say unto you, I will no more eat it (or: not) until it be fulfilled in the Kingdom of God.'

In the Lucan context this word can evidently only express the satisfaction of Jesus at having now been able to realize the desire. Luke could not have understood it otherwise since he follows the Marcan chronology. But let us isolate the verse from its Lucan context and consider it in itself. Then let us note this significant detail: Luke makes to follow it the declaration of Jesus on the fruit of the vine which he has borrowed from Mark. In Mark it was at the end of the narrative. Luke has placed it at the beginning of his account of the meal and it is clear that he wished to juxtapose these two declarations which seemed to him akin: 'And he received a cup, and when he had given thanks, he said: Take this, and divide it among yourselves: For I say unto you I will not drink from henceforth of the fruit of the vine, until the Kingdom of God shall come.' It would seem that Luke read the first statement of Jesus, which he must have got from some special written or oral tradition, in the light of the second reported by Mark. It is possible that the Greek phrasing of the second influenced the first, e.g. 'For I say unto you' ($\lambda\acute{\epsilon}\gamma\omega$ $\gamma\grave{\alpha}\rho$ $\acute{\nu}\mu\hat{\iota}\nu$). As for $o\grave{\nu}\kappa\acute{\epsilon}\tau\iota$ $o\grave{\nu}$ $\mu\acute{\eta}$ in v. 16 it might well come from Mark 14.25. A curious detail is that our text of Luke 22.18 has dropped the

---

[1] Delitzsch, Merx, Blakiston, Jouön, Schniewind.

οὐκέτι of Mark 14.25, and has replaced it by ἀπὸ τοῦ νῦν. No doubt Luke found too heavy the accumulation of three negatives. This makes it unlikely that Luke has piled up the three negatives in Luke 22.16. A rapid survey of the variants shows, moreover, that the majority of the best manuscripts do not have this οὐκέτι.[1] Besides the study of the variants shows in certain manuscripts a tendency to adjust Luke 22.16 to the parallel word about the fruit of the vine. Thus D has boldly put 'eat again' instead of 'be fulfilled', which seems to show that the copyist of D was shocked by the expression 'be fulfilled'. This corrector no doubt felt that the text which he had in front of him was incompatible with Luke's interpretation. Thus it is quite likely that the oldest text of Luke said simply οὐ μή = by no means. But even if this οὐκέτι was original it would not necessarily mean that Jesus had yet in reality eaten this passover. In disputing the hypothesis of Burkitt and Brooke,[2] who think that Jesus here expresses his regret at no longer being able to eat this passover, Lietzmann[3] bases his argument only on the fact that the context of Luke forbids this interpretation and thus he recognizes implicitly that taken by itself Luke 22.15 would well justify it. Jeremias,[4] too, can find no other argument.

It is thus very possible and even fairly probable that Luke has interpreted this word of Jesus in a tendencious manner. If then we read it apart from the preconceived idea of Luke it can mean just as well the regret at no longer being able to eat this passover. This interpretation is moreover much more logical. Whereas the word about the fruit of the vine is perfectly coherent, since Jesus declares at the moment of drinking it that he will not drink it again 'until I drink it *new* in the Kingdom of God' (Mark), the word about the Passover is incoherent in the interpretation of Luke. Of a Passover which he has in fact already eaten with his disciples he would rather have said that he would eat it again in the Kingdom. It is clear that the parallelism between these two words of Jesus is somewhat superficial: one can scarcely speak of a future fulfilment when a thing is realized already. And this

---

[1] Sinaiticus, Alexandrinus, Vaticanus, Codex Ephrem, Koridethi, the Lake group, the Coptic translations, *la vetus itala* and the Vulgate.
[2] *Journal of Theological Studies*, IX, 1908, pp. 569-572.
[3] *Messe und Herrnmahl*, Berlin, 1926, p. 206, note 1.
[4] *Die Abendmahlsworte* . . . , p. 7, note 2.

superficial parallelism has no doubt caused Luke to misunderstand the word about the Passover. Finally an attentive study of the two verses 15 and 16 shows that if Luke were right Jesus would pass suddenly from an atmosphere of satisfaction to one of sadness which, without being impossible, is psychologically less probable than our interpretation which finds in these verses the same sentiment of sadness and its consolation by the prospect of the heavenly feast.

Thus this word means that Jesus is sorrowful at having to die without having yet eaten this passover with his own.

But this observation is not yet sufficiently certain for us to be able to build on it alone the scaffolding of a solid hypothesis. Our verse contains a motif which seems to us important in a deeper way and which exegetes seem to have neglected so far. By saying that this Passover will be fulfilled in the Kingdom Jesus gives to the meal an eschatological sense. And this incontestable fact will provide a solid point of departure.

Whether Jesus really ate this passover or not it is certain that he established a connexion between this Paschal meal and the Messianic banquet in the Kingdom of God. Now as the last meal is doubtless an anticipation of the Kingdom—the word about the fruit of the vine and the Pauline tradition of I Cor. 11.26, '. . . till he come' amply proves it—Jesus might well have anticipated that evening not only the feast of the Kingdom in general but also the Paschal motives which this eschatological feast implied for him. If we take seriously the word 'fulfil' this interpretation is irresistible. But what were these 'motifs'? If we bear in mind the classical pattern of ideas which we find in our four Gospels and in the rest of the New Testament, as also in Jewish thought, a pattern according to which the time of the Exodus is an immense symbolic foreshadowing of the end of time, it is probable that these motifs are essentially those of the covenant and the blood which are just what we find in the words of institution as reported by Paul and Mark. Further, the imminence of the passover of the following day naturally facilitated the anticipation. But this imminence is not essential and would not in itself suffice to substantiate our hypothesis, which rests above all on the evident fact that Jesus here gives an eschatological meaning to the Passover.

We know that the Jewish Passover was not only a feast of memory turned towards the past but also a feast of hope looking towards the future and the great deliverance of Israel and the Kingdom of God. The idea of Jesus which forged a link between the Paschal feast and the Kingdom of God did not therefore present any difficulty in principle for his contemporaries. Again, is it not remarkable that the story of the Last Supper, like the Jewish Passover, has a Janus head? With Paul especially the terms 'in remembrance of me' seem to suggest the Paschal theme of remembrance which plays such a great part in the Paschal liturgy, and the words 'till he come', like the phrase about the fruit of the vine reported by Mark, are evocative of the future.

We cannot here enter into a detailed discussion, unfortunately, of the text and the meaning of the various accounts of the supper. But that is not essential for the limited purpose of these pages. There is reason to distinguish indeed between two quite different things: on the one hand the *fact* that Jesus sees in this Passover something which will be fulfilled in the Kingdom and introduces therefore into this last meal Paschal motives, and on the other the *question* of the extent and precise character of these motives. It is as difficult to reach behind the labyrinth of our texts a perfectly clear vision and complete certainty with regard to the second point as it is easy to establish the first.

We can thus leave aside the very complex question of the exact meaning and Paschal character of the motives concerning the blood and the covenant.[1] We can, if not separate, at least distinguish, and not confuse—as is still done in recent discussions—the chronological and theological problems. It is possible to decide the chronological point without the discussion leading to an unequivocal result in regard to the theological point. Further by proceeding thus we might be able to throw an unexpected light on the theological question.

In every branch of knowledge the value of a hypothesis may

[1] Let us note simply that the new covenant of Jer. 31.31 of which Jesus probably was thinking purposes to transcend and fulfil that of the exodus. The link with the Passover is evident: 'a new covenant not like the covenant which I made with their forefathers in the day when I took them by the hand to bring them out of Egypt . . . for I will pardon their iniquity and will no longer remember their sin' (vv. 32, 34). It will be noted that the covenant and the forgiveness of sins recall the idea of blood and sacrifice.

be measured by its internal coherence, but still more, perhaps, by its capacity to explain at one and the same time a whole series of divergent facts which appear incoherent and irreconcilable with each other. The hypothesis which we are here proposing, it would seem, enables us to explain the outstanding data of our conflicting traditions.

First it is in conformity with the too few indications given us by the oldest of our witnesses, the apostle Paul. He gives four short but quite precise notes:

(*a*) In his introduction to the words of institution I Cor. 11.23, an introduction which is not the invention of Paul but forms part of the oral tradition which he has received from the primitive Church, the apostle does not speak of a Passover evening, he says simply 'in the night in which he was betrayed'.

Three positive indications correspond to this negative one:

(*b*) In the same epistle, I Cor. 5.7, Paul keenly urges the Corinthian Church to 'purge out the old leaven, that ye may be a new lump, even as ye are unleavened. For our Passover also hath been sacrificed, even Christ.' This witness is precise. The apostle does not see in the Christ a new Moses who has instituted in the Eucharist a new edition of the Passover. Even the Synoptics which at first sight seem inevitably to tend towards this idea, and Luke in particular, do not go far in this direction. This idea is excluded not only at the end of the first century by the Johannine tradition, but also right from the first decades of the Church's life by the formal witness of Paul: Christ died as a veritable Paschal Lamb, he was immolated as a sacrifice ($\dot{\epsilon}\tau\dot{v}\theta\eta$).

(*c*) In this same passage, I Cor. 5.6-8, which should be understood as a unity, Paul does not give two disconnected allegories, one on the proverb 'a little leaven leaveneth the whole lump', the other on Christ our Passover. The special aim of the apostle is to remind the Corinthians that their church is unleavened bread and a new lump. The Church is a new creation; it must be worthy of the new aeon. This metaphor, the Church = unleavened bread, becomes less puzzling if we take seriously what the apostle writes a little further on to the same Corinthians, I Cor. 10.16-17: 'The bread which we break is it not a communion of the Body of

Christ? Seeing that we who are many, are one bread, one body. For we all partake of the one bread.' As the Body of Christ, the Church can thus be very properly called also unleavened bread, the pure bread of the new age.

Paul has thus associated and even intermingled in a way which may seem strange to us but which we can only accept as a fact the Passover, the new aeon, Christ as Paschal sacrifice, the bread of the Eucharist, the Church as the Body of Christ. These associations of ideas have no meaning evidently except against the background of that immense vision in which the Exodus, the Paschal time, is seen as a huge symbolic foreshadowing of something which will be and is already being realized by the new creation.[1] That is precisely what the apostle partially amplifies in his great exhortation of I Cor. 10, which takes it for granted that all the narratives of the Exodus and the desert are a symbolic allusion to the sacraments and the Church of the end of the age.

(*d*) Lastly there is reason to emphasize that the 'cup of blessing' (*cos habberakah*) of I Cor. 10.16, and the motive of remembrance of I Cor. 11.24 suggest the Paschal liturgy—it suffices to read again Ex. 12.14, and the formula of benediction for the feast day in the Paschal liturgy: '. . . This feast day of unleavened bread, a remembrance (*zikaron*) of our deliverance.'

Thus the Pauline tradition contains clearly the two sets of facts: chronologically the meal was not Paschal; theologically it was so as a result of the death of Jesus, various associations of Paschal ideas and allusions to the Paschal liturgy.

Then our hypothesis is of course—no need to insist on the

---

[1] We may wonder whether the Jews did not associate the Passover with the new age too by reason of the fact that the month Nisan was the first month of their religious year. We have not in hand at the moment the data which would allow us to confirm or to repudiate this hypothesis. However that may be, the Passover evoked the new age, the *'olam habba*. Our colleague and friend Edmund Jacob points out to us this very significant text of Pesachim x, 6*c*, which throws light on the saying of Jesus about the Passover fulfilled in the Kingdom. Rabbi Agiba says: 'Thus Yahweh our God and the God of our fathers brings us to the feasts which signify for us our salvation, gladdening us with the building of the new age (*bebinjan colam*), to eat Paschal sacrifices and sacrifices whose blood sprinkles the side of thy altar to be pleasing to thee, and we praise thee for our deliverance.' It will be noted that the Paschal sacrifices and others (*pesakhim* and *zebakhim*), and the blood, are here associated in a way which is not very clear, but is certainly associated with the world to come.

point—in conformity with Johannine chronology. But chronology is not everything with John: when he sees in the Christ the Paschal Lamb whose bones were not broken (19.36), and who died for the sins of the world (1.29), John associates himself with the thought of Paul. And since nothing suggests here more than anywhere else that John is dependent on Paul—his terminology is too different not to be independent—inversely the Pauline tradition confirms that of John.

In particular we find in John, expressed in quite different terms but analogous in substance, a similar association of ideas to that of Paul, and linking the Passover, the manna of the Exodus, and the manna of the end of the age, to be brought by the second Saviour (*goël akharon*) the death of the Son of Man and the bread of the Last Supper. The whole of chapter 6 is placed by John under the sign of the approaching Passover: to enter into the new world it is necessary as formerly to have bread flesh and blood (Ex. 12.7, 8, 13, 46). In his fine commentary[1] Edwyn Hoskyns observes quite rightly: 'The movement from the miracle to the discourse, from Moses to Jesus (v. 32-35; cf. 1.17) and above all from bread to flesh is almost unintelligible unless the reference in v. 4 to the passover picks up 1.29, 36, anticipates 19.36 (Ex. 12.14; Num. 9.12) and governs the whole narrative.'

The Son of Man come down from heaven as a true prophet superior to Moses does not institute a second edition of the ancient rite; nor does he repeat the miracle of Moses; he does both less and more; he fulfils all that this great past had been able merely to suggest, he is in some way the true Passover. He does not give a heavenly abstract food detachable from his Person. He does not merely give, he *is* the bread of life. And this bread of life is not even his Person, his metaphysical being. This bread of life is the gift of the life of the Son of Man who has come down from heaven or, what comes to the same thing and is perhaps more accurate, he is the Son of Man giving himself and dying for the life of the world. Here there is an evident connexion with the theme of John 3.14-16, where the gift of life and the exaltation of the Son of Man are considered as the fulfilment of the ancient episode concerning the brazen serpent lifted up by Moses in the desert. All these themes which seem to

[1] *The Fourth Gospel*, London, 1942, vol. I, p. 315; cf. p. 325.

us associated and intermingled in a somewhat incoherent manner nevertheless fit very well into the context of the Last Supper as it emerges in Luke 22.15-16 and in Paul: allusions to the Exodus and the Passover spring up almost everywhere, because it is the totality of the events of the Exodus centring on the Passover which constitutes an enormous symbol realized in Jesus Christ. Let us add that the apostle Paul is not far from the Johannine theme of the Son of Man the Bread of Life. When he sees in the rock of the desert which poured out spiritual drink the Christ himself he may well have discerned the Christ also behind the spiritual food, the manna of the desert.

It will perhaps be objected that we are confusing too casually the Passover and the rest of the Exodus. We think that it is rather our modern mentality which is too fond of making distinctions. For the modern reader, especially if he has the good or bad fortune to be a historian, the story of the Passover is only a certain episode narrated in Ex. 12. For a Jew of the time of Jesus the point of view was very different. The annual Passover was the Jewish feast *par excellence*. Each time he celebrated it according to the famous rabbinical dictum, he was expected to think of himself as leaving Egypt. The rite evoked the whole cycle of that past deliverance—and also that which was to come. The father of the family explained to his children the meaning of the rite and recalled the various graces of the Exodus. And are not liturgical associations of ideas far more deeply alive and inspiring for us men than a consistent historical narrative? If they make do with somewhat crude logical links they are none the less powerful for that. Thus modern exegetes exaggerate perhaps the difficulty raised by the mention of the blood of the covenant in Mark 14.24. The expression comes in fact from the covenant of Sinai (Ex. 24.8) and has nothing to do in strict logic with the Passover. But everything leads us to believe that Jesus and the men of his time were less smitten with the passion for historical precision than ourselves and saw rather in the stories of the Exodus a totality which, because of their liturgical customs, was simply a development of the theme of the Passover.

Besides, our modern perspective is deeply distorted by our traditional ideas about the sacraments. The word sacrament suggests to us in the first place the idea of an institution, the old problem of the relation between a rite and its meaning, between form and matter, spiritual reality and substance, etc. There is only one shade of meaning which is hidden from or only with difficulty noted by our modern outlook and this is just the element which in the New Testament is basic: the eschatological character and meaning of the sacrament. The latter was not a rite which had its meaning and efficacy in itself. It derives these from the past and still more from the future, from that world to come which will fulfil all promises and types of ancient days. The Eucharist in particular could not possibly be an institution. It could only be so if it were an autonomous rite conferring a special grace.

Now it does but sum up in a few gestures and words the *whole* gift implied in the life and death of the Son of Man. Of course Jesus instituted the Last Supper; but not by a sort of juridical, autonomous and abstract act of foundation. He instituted it by the whole of his life, and especially by his death and resurrection.[1] And it will not be fully accomplished until the time of the Parousia in the great communion of the Kingdom, at the table of the Father. In celebrating the festal meal, Jesus and his disciples are in a way on the threshold of the new world: already the past of the Exodus is completed in Jesus and yet the present and this past will be fully consummated only in the Kingdom. It is in this tension between the world of the past and that of the life to come that the Supper is situated—as also is the Baptism. It is this tension which the sacraments enable one to endure and to overcome. For the early Christians the sacraments are much less a victory over the gulf between spirit and matter—that is what they have become, alas, through the centuries, whence so many pseudo-problems and false alternatives—than a conquest of the temporal tension between the present aeon and that which is to come in Jesus Christ. Obsessed by the question of the relation

[1] The same may be said of the foundation of the Church. One institutes a rite in the pagan sense of the word. One institutes an association a foundation or a club which will date from such a day and such an hour. If critics had begun by analysing closely what the word 'Church' means in the texts, as K. L. Schmidt has done in the *Festgabe für Deissmann*, Tübingen, 1927, 2. Aufl. des Sonderdruckes, 1932, and in his article in the ThWBNT, they would have seen that to wish to assign to a particular word or act of Jesus the foundation of the Church is a work of Sisyphus, in that the body of the Son of Man, the Church, is both the true Israel of all times, and the new collective man who cannot be created except by the totality of the life, death and resurrection of the Son of Man.

between the living Christ and the elements of bread and wine, we pose the problem in terms of space rather than time, which are more Hellenistic than Biblical, as if the Eucharist were but a non-temporal rite actualizing the myth of a mystery religion, and we are incapable of grasping the fact that the problem must be viewed less in terms of space than of time.

The meaning of the Eucharist cannot therefore be limited to the question of the words of institution, although they are central and essential. It is much richer: it includes manifold allusions, varied correspondences with both the past and the future, since it is the totality of the process of salvation which is concentrated there and given to the faithful. Hence passages like I Cor. 10 or John 6 are by no means in substance, even if they are in form, illegitimate typological extensions of the primary meaning of the Supper. As a Jew of that time Jesus must have known and given utterance to such associations of ideas. And I Cor. 10 and John 6 only disclose partial glimpses into this whole corpus of rich and complex motifs which the Supper implied from the start.

That is why John was able to omit the story of the institution of the Eucharist. Doubtless the words of institution were well known; they must very soon have constituted the framework of the liturgy as well as its justification. The Marcan account looks very much less like a historical document than a short extract drawn up by the early Church for its catechetical and liturgical purposes. It is not at all surprising that this extract is short and somewhat thin. This was necessary to produce a firm stable tradition required to be authoritative. It cannot be too much emphasized that the Marcan account is hardly more circumstantial than the tradition of the Church which Paul recalls to the Corinthians in I Cor. 11! Once more, Mark yields, concerning the Last Supper of Jesus, only this meagre liturgical extract. It is not sufficiently noticed that the central idea of the Supper, the evocation of the feast in the Kingdom, is only lightly touched on in the story by the reference to the fruit of the vine. In order to know more about this Last Supper, at which it is grotesque to suppose that Jesus said no more for the rest of the evening, we should have to look elsewhere.

Above all John can be content to allude to the Last Supper in chapter 13 because the meaning of the Eucharist amply exceeds the words of institution. A close analysis shows that further Eucharistic motives are to be found elsewhere.[1] In chapter 6 John reports Eucharistic themes which look very much as if they were authentic in substance if not in form. As for John 13, where many critics deny any connexion with the Supper, we hope to show soon that the foot-washing bears an eschatological sense. In fact the parable of Luke 12.35-37, where the master returning from the marriage becomes the servant of his servants and treats them as friends, has meaning only if the Son of Man returning in his Parousia reverses the order of this world and manifests his glory by becoming the servant of his own. Thus the Son of Man will be servant not only in his life and death but even in his Kingdom where he will treat his elect as friends. Then to reign and to serve will be one and the same. In the light of this text, Luke 22.27, 'I am in the midst of you as he that serveth', and the account of John 13 throw light on each other: the Son of Man anticipates the great feast of the Kingdom. He gives not only a sign of his love and humility which carries him to the point of dying as a servant for his friends but at the same time a demonstration of the law of the Kingdom which will be to love and to serve. Thus the ceaseless discussions as to whether the Supper is a sad memorial of the death of Jesus or a joyful eschatological anticipation of the great heavenly feast—we are at last beginning to realize that we are discussing a false problem[2]— become pointless. The continuity is perfect: the idea of the Son of Man serving on earth by the gift of his life and in his Kingdom at the table of his father obliges us to see the glory and the joy of the Kingdom already mysteriously present and real in the Last Supper. To serve and to reign are wonderfully identical. Hence we understand better the solemn declaration of Jesus: 'Now is the Son of man glorified, and God is glorified in him' (John 13.31). Thus we can grasp better the Johannine confusion— very deliberate moreover—between abasement and glorification, exaltation on the Cross and exaltation at the Father's side, between the obscure present and the glorious future.

If the hypothesis which we have just suggested is true it is

---

[1] Cf. O. Cullmann, *Les sacrements dans l'Evangile johannique*, Paris, 1951.
[2] Ed. Schweizer, Das Abendmahl eine Vergegenwärtigung des Todes Jesu oder ein eschatologisches Freudenmahl? ThZ 1946/2, pp. 81-100.

certain that John 13 refers indeed to the Supper, the eschatological feast. The foot-washing and the words of Jesus which comment on it contain the two essential elements of the Eucharist: that the Son of Man has not come to be ministered to but to minister, and to give his life, and that he will receive and serve his own at the table in the Kingdom. They will have part with him (John 13.8), they will occupy the places which he has prepared for them (John 14.3 and Luke 22.27-28), when once again he is in the bosom of the Father (John 1.18), reclining at the place of honour at the table of the Father.

Thus while waiting for the day of his final and glorious return the disciples will live among themselves by the law of love and service which is indispensable in the house of the Father. Like the liturgy of the *Didache* John can speak of the Supper without mentioning the words of institution and the elements.

But let us return to the analysis of our various traditions while retaining only from this digression an impression of the narrowness of the traditional concepts in which again and again we try to squeeze the rich and polyphonic motifs of the Supper.

So long as we do not enlarge the horizon and break with the prejudice that the account of the institution is the alpha and omega of the Eucharist, the various strands of the tradition will remain an incoherent puzzle. But so soon as we recognize that the words of institution are only the centre around which revolve other elements, it becomes possible to recover not only the richness but also the internal coherence of the Supper. The exegete must listen to the texts with a musician's ear in order to perceive not merely the dominant melody but also the underlying polyphony.

Having found in both John and Paul the two series of facts: on the hand the chronological indications suggesting that Jesus died on the eve of the Passover and preventing us from supposing that the meal was a Paschal meal, on the other the theological Paschal motives of the Eucharist, we must now return to the witness of the Synoptics.

How shall we account for the chronology of Mark, so faithfully followed by Matthew and Luke? It seems to us that the rise and spread of this mistaken chronology is relatively easy to explain.

If any association with the Passover had been quite alien to the Last Supper of Jesus, it would certainly be impossible to account for the rise of this chronology. The mistake would have been so much cruder as the primitive Church still continued for a long time to celebrate each year the Jewish Passover (cf. Acts 20.6). Lietzmann, who emphasizes this fact,[1] notes that 'this annual feast could not have been identified either in meaning or rite with the Last Supper'.

This coexistence of Passover and Eucharist in the custom of the primitive Church would have made very difficult the chronological assimilation of the Last Supper with a Paschal meal. Any confusion or contamination could not have resulted from a liturgical synchronization.

The ease with which the first Christians continued to celebrate the Jewish Passover suggests on the contrary that they did not see in the last meal of Jesus a second edition of the Jewish festival which, coinciding with it in point of time, duplicated it and needed to be distinguished from it.

And we find no such suggestion in the texts, which say that it is the death of Jesus and the new world which it opens to the faithful that form the true fulfilment of the Jewish feast. And it is doubtless because this confusion was impossible that Luke has not in essence assimilated the Paschal feast (Luke 22.15-17) and the Supper (Luke 22.18-20).

Hence if Mark or the tradition which he reflects could have seen in the Last Supper a Paschal meal it must have had some feature which might have given occasion to such an interpretation. Further if the last meal of Jesus did in fact contain Paschal motifs it is easy to understand what happened. Not only the meagre liturgical extract preserved by Paul and Mark but also the memories which oral tradition must have cherished for several decades were too laden with Paschal associations not to culminate quite naturally in the almost inevitable schematization: Meal with a Paschal theme! Then Paschal meal!

It goes without saying that the primitive Church was more concerned with theology than with chronology. It is even surprising that this confusion did not extend to the whole story. It seems that history defended itself against the schematization. Let

---

[1] *Messe und Herrnmahl*, pp. 211-212.

us say rather that history would probably have yielded if it had not been kept intact by the deep faithful interpretation of the supper given by the apostle Paul, John, and doubtless a part of Church tradition: not a mechanical correspondence between the new rite and the old, but a fulfilment in Christ of all that the ancient rite sought to embody and symbolize.

On this point as on many others the firmness of the Christo-centric thought of the early Church, in which the mania of modern critics sees too readily a factor of distortion, has in fact preserved the tradition and saved the reality of history.

Besides, the error of the Synoptics did not go deep: only their chronology is mistaken. The substance of the Marcan narrative about the Last Supper has in its external features no connexion with the Passover and this has often been noted. It is merely the editorial framework which has been influenced by the schemati-zation. It is true that we have the story of Jesus sending the two disciples to prepare the Passover. In the form in which we read it in Mark, Matthew and Luke, the story can only be a subsequent arrangement, an attempt to reconstruct the course of events. But even in this patchwork there may be a nucleus of historical fact: for it expresses admirably the very keen desire of Jesus to eat once more the passover with his friends before suffering. And this desire, already attested by the ancient tradition reflected in Luke 22.15, justifies us in thinking that it is not impossible that Jesus, feeling the growing crisis of events, wished to foresee and arrange things twenty-four hours in advance. In that case the margin of error involved in the tradition represented by Mark would be further reduced.

This supposition would enable us to explain a rather serious difficulty: the tradition, both Johannine and Synoptic, is at one in representing both Jesus and his disciples as *reclining* at the table and not seated. It is known that in order to mark their own supremacy the Jews had adopted for solemn feasts the custom of their masters: at the Passover it was essential to *recline*, in the Kingdom, the elect will *recline* at table. Mark tells us that the room was furnished and prepared (ἐστρωμένον). John 13 pre-supposes that the disciples are reclining since the beloved disciple is lying in the bosom of Jesus (13.23), i.e. reclining on his right hand. Jesus lies down again, v. 12, cf. v. 28.

Since for John the meal was not a Passover, and thus there was no reason to be reclining, the most logical supposition is that the meal took place in the room prepared for the Paschal feast of the following day. The fact of the reclining position also facilitated the anticipation of the eschatological Paschal meal.

Luke alone, who likes to be consistent, seems to have tried to mould the substance of the story according to the pattern of the Passover ritual. Hence no doubt the two cups. But he did not go far in this direction: he speaks neither of unleavened bread nor of the Paschal lamb nor of liturgical prayers nor of the explanation of the rite by the president at the feast. One has rather the impression that Luke, anxious to give logical structure to his data without adding anything of his own,[1] has simply arranged his material so as to suggest first the Paschal meal and then to give the traditional account of the Supper. Or is it possible that Jesus imparted to the meal certain external features of the Passover, the use of the two cups in particular? This seems unlikely. Without Paschal Lamb or unleavened bread the rite would have been too much truncated. Let us suppose rather with Dibelius that by filling out his story with sayings such as Luke 22.15-16, 25-32, 35, 38, which circulated in isolation, Luke has tried to give a fuller account of this meal which he believed to have been a Passover. He borrowed from the end of Mark's story the saying about the fruit of the vine, introduced it by a first cup of wine and thus obtained both a rather fine parallelism with the word about the Passover being fulfilled in the Kingdom and a beginning of a Paschal meal with more than one cup. But in what follows there is nothing further to recall externally a Paschal meal. Luke has succeeded only in juxtaposing with the Eucharist the beginnings of a Passover celebration.

These two cups greatly puzzled the copyists of the first centuries who were familiar only with the one cup of the Christian liturgy. The discordant voices of the variants show eloquently how they were at pains by various methods to reduce the cups to one. The famous short text of *Codex D*, which till quite recently almost all exegetes considered to be nearest to historical

---

[1] M. Dibelius, *Die Formgeschichte des Evangeliums*, 2. Aufl. Tübingen, 1933, p. 212, note 2.

reality, has just received some shattering blows which might well have the effect of dethroning it. Following the offensive of Gaugler,[1] Ed. Schweizer[2] has just shown that the Alexandrine text—the one given by our Bibles—must be the earliest. To the old argument of Merx who contended against the partisans of D how the various Syriac witnesses had also felt obliged to make desperate attempts to reduce the cups to one, he adds the very pertinent observation that Tatian and Marcion in the second century had known only a text of the Alexandrine type. All that we have just been arguing points evidently in the same direction.

The partisans of the short text of *Codex D* (Luke 22.15-19*a*), who consider that his account, which they believe to be the most authentic, is unaware of the allusion to the covenant and the blood (of Pauline provenance) do not seem to have noticed a contradiction which seriously compromises their theory. The alternative is: either the allusion to the Passover, Luke 22.15-16, of their authentic text has a meaning, in which case it must be admitted that the rest of the story contains Paschal motives, which can only be the covenant and the blood mentioned in the Alexandrine text; or these verses have no meaning and they must be arbitrarily cut out. Whatever be our opinion, the short text of D is a truncated and incoherent account, and we must choose. After all that precedes we can but decide in favour of the Alexandrine text.[3]

But as a thorough study of all the aspects of the problem would take us far beyond the restricted area of this study let us simply note that the hypothesis we have proposed would enable us to establish a synthesis, perhaps, not only of the various data of the traditions but also of recent scholarly works. In order not to lengthen and make burdensome these pages we have avoided engaging in a discussion with Jeremias, Behm (ThWbNT

[1] *Das Abendmahl im Neuen Testament*, Basle, 1943.
[2] *Das Abendmahl eine Vergegenwärtigung . . .* , *art. cit.*, p. 86.
[3] In the American review, *Anglican Theological Review*, 1948, No. 1, pp. 56-57, B. H. Throckmorton ('The longer reading of Luke 22.19*b*-20') supports the Alexandrine text with arguments which coincide with ours. He rightly criticizes the fact that the authors of the new Revised Standard Version of the New Testament, published in 1946 in the U.S.A.—which in other respects seems to us excellent —have relegated to a note the long text of Luke 22.15-20.

article κλάω), Gaugler, Markus Barth,[1] and Ed. Schweizer. Their works have the merit, among other things, of establishing the vital role of Paschal motives in this Last Supper of Jesus. But their weakness lies in the fact that they have not solved the problems raised by the chronology of Mark. In the Last Supper of Jesus we are not faced with the stark alternative—either a feast which is chronologically a Passover or an ordinary meal without Paschal character: *tertium datur!*

[1] Markus Barth, *Das Abendmahl Passahmahl, Bundesmahl und Messiasmahl (Theol. Studien,* 18), Zollikon-Zurich, 1945. It is a great pity that in this work we find among so many true and really suggestive insights, methods of exegesis and speculations which are so risky and uncalled for. Yet M. Barth has the great merit, after Cullmann and Gaugler, of significantly widening the horizon of the ordinary Protestant view of the Last Supper. But is that a reason for minimizing at all the importance of the anamnesis of the death of Jesus and thus needing the energetic reminder of I Cor. 11.26-34? *In extremis* we receive the volume of Fr. J. Leenhardt, *Le Sacrement de la Sainte Cène,* Neuchâtel-Paris, 1948. Chapter 2 bears the same title as our article. After discussing various classical hypotheses the author leaves undecided the chronological question and remarks with justice that 'the Paschal interpretation of the Last Supper of Jesus does not appear to us to depend immediately on the solution of the chronological problem' (p. 14). As for the rest of the book, which deals somewhat with all the problems of exegesis and history which have any bearing on the Supper, we cannot discuss it here. Chapter 3, on the meaning of the Passover, shows very well the richness and the importance of the associations of ideas suggested by the Jewish Passover. On the other hand Chapter 9, on the Gospel of John, seems to us less felicitous and confines itself to John 6 without even discussing the ideas of Hoskyns, for example, and of Cullmann.

INDEX OF BIBLICAL REFERENCES